DEPARTMENT OF DEFENSE (DoD)
CLOUD COMPUTING
SECURITY REQUIREMENTS GUIDE (SRG)

12 January 2015

Trademark Information

Names, products, and services referenced within this document may be the trade names, trademarks, or service marks of their respective owners. References to commercial vendors and their products or services are provided strictly as a convenience to our users, and do not constitute or imply endorsement by DoD, DISA, or DISA Field Security Operations (FSO) of any non-Federal entity, event, product, service, or enterprise.

Table of Contents

List of Tables

List of Figures

UNCLASSIFIED

This page is intentionally blank.

UNCLASSIFIED

1   INTRODUCTION

Cloud computing technology and services provide the Department of Defense (DoD) with the opportunity to deploy an Enterprise Cloud Environment aligned with Federal Department-wide Information Technology (IT) strategies and efficiency initiatives, including federal data center consolidation. Cloud computing enables the Department to consolidate infrastructure, leverage commodity IT functions, and eliminate functional redundancies while improving continuity of operations. The overall success of these initiatives depends upon well executed security requirements, defined and understood by both DoD Components and industry. Consistent implementation and operation of these requirements assures mission execution, provides sensitive data protection, increases mission effectiveness, and ultimately results in the outcomes and operational efficiencies the DoD seeks.

The 15 December 2014 DoD CIO memo regarding *Updated Guidance on the Acquisition and Use of Commercial Cloud Computing Services* defines DoD Component responsibilities when acquiring commercial cloud services. The memo allows components to responsibly acquire cloud services minimally in accordance with the security requirements outlined in Federal Risk and Authorization Management Program (FedRAMP) FedRAMP and this Security Requirement Guide (SRG). DISA previously published the concepts for operating in the commercial cloud under the Cloud Security Model. Version 1 defined the overall framework and provided initial guidance for public data. Version 2.1 added information for Controlled Unclassified Information. This document, the Cloud Computing Security Requirements Guide (SRG), documents cloud security requirements in a construct similar to other SRGs published by DISA for the DoD. This SRG incorporates, supersedes, and rescinds the previously published Cloud Security Model.

The following terms will be used throughout this document:
- CSP by itself refers to any or all Cloud Service Providers, DoD or non-DoD.
- Non-DoD CSP will refer to a commercial or Federal Government owned and operated CSP.
- Commercial CSP will refer to a Non-DoD Non-Federal Government organization offering cloud services to the public and/or government customers as a business, typically for a fee with the intent to make a profit.
- DoD CSP will refer to a DoD owned and operated CSP.
- CSO refers to a CSP's Cloud Service Offering (recognizing that a CSP may have multiple offerings).
- Commercial Cloud Service is a CSO offered by a Commercial CSP.
- Mission Owners are entities such as program managers within the DoD Components responsible for instantiating information systems and applications leveraging a CSP's Cloud Service Offering.

1.1   Purpose and Audience

FedRAMP is a Federal Government program focused on enabling secure cloud computing for the Federal Government. DoD, by the virtue of its warfighting mission, has unique information protection requirements that extend beyond the controls assessed via FedRAMP. This document outlines the security controls and additional requirements necessary for using cloud-based solutions within the DoD.

The Cloud Computing SRG serves several purposes:

- Provides security requirements and guidance to non-DoD owned and operated Cloud Service Providers (CSPs) that wish to have their service offerings included in the DoD Cloud Service Catalog[1].
- Establishes a basis on which DoD will assess the security posture of a non-DoD CSP's service offering, supporting the decision to grant a DoD Provisional Authorization (PA) that allows a non-DoD CSP to host DoD missions.
- Defines the policies, requirements, and architectures for the use and implementation of commercial cloud services by DoD Mission Owners.
- Provides guidance to DoD Mission Owners and Assessment and Authorization officials (formerly Certification and Accreditation) in planning and authorizing the use of a CSP.

The audience for this Cloud Computing SRG includes:

- Commercial and non-DoD Federal Government CSPs
- DoD programs operating as a CSP
- DoD Components and Mission Owners using, or considering the use of, commercial/non-DoD and DoD cloud computing services
- DoD risk management assessment officials and Authorizing Officials (AOs)

1.2 Authority

This document is provided under the authority of DoD Instruction 8500.01 and DoD Instruction 8510.01.

DoDI 8500.01, entitled Cybersecurity, directs Director DISA, under the authority, direction, and control of the DoD CIO to develop and maintain Control Correlation Identifiers (CCIs), Security Requirements Guides (SRGs), Security Technical Implementation Guides (STIGs), and mobile code risk categories and usage guides that implement and are consistent with DoD cybersecurity policies, standards, architectures, security controls, and validation procedures, with the support of the NSA/CSS, using input from stakeholders, and using automation whenever possible.

DoDI 8500.01 further directs DoD Component heads to ensure that all DoD Information Technologies (IT) under their purview comply with applicable STIGs, [NSA] security configuration guides, and SRGs with any exceptions documented and approved by the responsible Authorizing Official (AO).

DoDI 8510.01 implements NIST SP 800-37, NIST SP 800-53, Committee on National Security Systems (CNSS) Instruction (CNSSI) 1253, and the Federal Information Security Management Act (FISMA) by establishing the DoD Risk Management Framework (RMF) for DoD IT, establishing associated cybersecurity policy, and assigning responsibilities for executing and maintaining the RMF.

---

[1] DoD Cloud Service Catalog:
https://disa.deps.mil/disa/org/atb/Cloud%20Broker/Lists/Catalog/CatalogPageView.aspx (DoD PKI required)

UNCLASSIFIED

1.3   Scope and Applicability

This Cloud Computing SRG establishes the DoD security objectives to host DoD missions up to and including SECRET on CSOs. Missions above SECRET must follow existing applicable DoD policies and are not covered by this SRG.

This SRG applies to all CSP offerings, regardless of who owns or operates the environments. This SRG also applies to any supporting cloud service provider or facilities provider that a CSP might leverage to provide a complete service. While the CSP's overall service offering may be inheriting controls and compliance from a third party, the prime CSP is ultimately responsible for complete compliance.

The assessment of security controls and other DoD requirements for commercial and non-DoD CSPs is based the use of FedRAMP, supplemented with DoD considerations as outlined in section 4 of this document. DoD enterprise service programs providing cloud capabilities or service offerings (e.g. milCloud, Defense Enterprise Email) use DoD's assessment and authorization process under the DoD RMF. Both processes utilize the NIST SP 800-53 security controls as the basis of the assessment; providing a common framework under which DoD can determine the level of risk.

This SRG establishes the DoD baseline security requirements for DoD Mission Owners when contracting for and using non-DoD Software as a Service (SaaS) offering, and when implementing their systems and applications on DoD or non- DoD Infrastructure as a Service (IaaS) and Platform as a Service (PaaS) offerings. Since IaaS and PaaS involve CSP customers building a system or application on top of these service offerings, this SRG considers IaaS and PaaS as being similar and treats them in the same manner, unless stated otherwise. SaaS is addressed to the extent of the other service models, with specific application requirements being identified in other application-related SRGs and STIGs.

1.4   Security Requirements Guides (SRGs) / Security Technical Implementation Guides (STIGs)

Security Requirements Guides (SRGs) are collections of requirements applicable to a given technology family, product category, or an organization in general. SRGs provide non-product specific requirements to mitigate sources of security vulnerabilities consistently and commonly encountered across IT systems and applications.

While the SRGs define the high level requirements for various technology families and organizations, the Security Technical Implementation Guides (STIGs) are the detailed guidelines for specific products. In other words, STIGs provide product-specific information for validating, attaining, and continuously maintaining compliance with requirements defined in the SRG for that product's technology area.

A single technology related SRG or STIG is not all inclusive for a given system. Compliance with all SRGs/STIGs applicable to the system is required. This may result in a given system being subject to multiple SRGs and/or STIGs.

Newly published STIGs generally consist of a technology/product overview document and one or more .xml files in Extensible Configuration Checklist Description Format (XCCDF) containing the security requirements. Security requirements are presented in the form of Control Correlation Identifiers (CCIs) and include product specific configuration and validation procedures. Requirements in this SRG are not being published in an XCCDF XML format at this time.

The security requirements contained within SRGs and STIGs, in general, are applicable to all DoD-administered systems, all systems connected to DoD networks, and all systems operated and/or administrated on behalf of the DoD.

1.5 SRG and STIG Distribution

Interested parties can obtain the applicable SRGs and STIGs from the Information Assurance Support Environment (IASE) website. The unclassified website is http://iase.disa.mil and the classified website is http://iase.disa.smil.mil.

NOTE: Some content requires a PKI certificate for access. The IASE web site does NOT currently accept ECA certificates for entry into the PKI-protected area. Industry partners needing PKI restricted content may request it through their DoD sponsor.

1.6 Document Revisions and Update Cycle

DISA FSO develops, revises, updates, and publishes SRG and STIG documents in accordance with the DISA FSO quarterly maintenance release schedule. These publications reflect new or changed policies, requirements, threats, or mitigations; reorganize content; correct errors; and/or, provide additional clarity. The fiscal year based release schedule can be found at http://iase.disa.mil/stigs/Pages/fso-schedule.aspx.

Major updates to a SRG or STIG result in a version change rather than an incremental release. New SRGs and STIGs and major updates will be released as soon as they are approved and ready for publication at any time during the year.

Comments, proposed revisions, and questions are accepted via email at disa.letterkenny.FSO.mbx.stig-customer-support-mailbox@mail.mil. DISA Field Security Operations (FSO) coordinates all change requests with relevant DoD organizations before inclusion.

1.7 Document Organization

This SRG is organized into six major sections with supporting appendices. Sections 1-4 address general information including the processes for authorizing a particular CSP's cloud offering. Remaining sections outline specific security requirements to be addressed in authorizing and operating cloud capabilities. In addition to specifics on SRG roles and responsibilities, and required control parameter values, the appendices provide the references and definitions used throughout the document.

Section 1 – Introduction: Provides general information on the purpose and use of this document.

Section 2 – Background: Contains a primer on several terms and supporting concepts used throughout the document.

Section 3 – Impact Levels and Security Objectives: Explains the concept of "Impact Levels" based on the type of data being hosted in the cloud and outlines security objective considerations in the areas of Confidentiality, Integrity, and Availability.

Section 4 – Risk Assessment of Cloud Service Offerings: Provides an overview of the assessment and authorization processes used for granting a DoD provisional authorization (PA) and explains how a PA can be leveraged by a Mission Owner and its Authorizing Official (AO) in support of an Authority to Operate (ATO) decision.

Section 5 – Security Requirements: Details the requirements associated with enabling CSP capabilities.

Section 6 – Computer Network Defense and Incident Response: Outlines the requirements for defending information systems operating in the cloud along with the Command and Control (C2) processes necessary to defend and operate DoD mission systems.

This page is intentionally blank.

2   BACKGROUND

This section outlines several concepts, terms, and supporting processes, providing a primer for the remainder of this document.

2.1   Cloud Computing, Cloud Service, and Cloud Deployment Models

The National Institute of Standards and Technology (NIST) Special Publication (SP) 800-145[2] defines cloud computing, five essential characteristics, three service models, and four deployment models. This SRG adheres to these NIST definitions to characterize and standardize the discussion of Cloud Computing.

> *"Cloud computing is a model for enabling ubiquitous, convenient, on-demand network access to a shared pool of configurable computing resources (e.g., networks, servers, storage, applications, and services) that can be rapidly provisioned and released with minimal management effort or service provider interaction."*

Cloud service models include Software as a Service (SaaS), Platform as a Service (PaaS), and Infrastructure as a Service (IaaS). The components offered in IaaS form the basis for PaaS, while the components offered in PaaS form the basis of SaaS. Cloud deployment models include Public, Private, Community, and Hybrid. Please see NIST SP 800-145 for the detailed definitions of these models.

While vendors may market and name their offerings as they wish, DISA will categorize them into one of the three NIST cloud service models when listing them in the DoD Cloud Service Catalog. Vendors are encouraged to market their services using the NIST cloud service models. Service offerings that provide data storage without also providing computing services will be considered to be a subset of IaaS.As used in this SRG the terms cloud computing and cloud services refer to service offering from a provider organization to one or more organizational customers or tenant organizations. These terms do not refer to classic forms of IT services delivery where dedicated hardware (whether it is virtualized or not) is employed or assembled by organizations for their own use. A service offering from a provider organization to a customer must be part of the construct.

2.2   Cloud Service Provider (CSP) and Cloud Service Offering (CSO)

A Cloud Service Provider (CSP) is an entity that offers one or more cloud services in one or more deployment models. A CSP might leverage or outsource services of other organizations and other CSPs (e.g., placing certain servers or equipment in third party facilities such as data centers, carrier hotels / collocation facilities, and Internet Network Access Points (NAPs)). CSPs offering SaaS may leverage one or more third party CSP's (i.e., for IaaS or PaaS) to build out a capability or offering.

A Cloud Service Offering (CSO) is the actual IaaS/PaaS/SaaS solution available from a CSP. This distinction is important since a CSP may provide several different CSOs.

---

[2] NIST SP 800-145: http://csrc.nist.gov/publications/PubsSPs.html

2.3 DoD Risk Management Framework (DoD RMF)

DoDI 8510.01 is the implementing policy for the DoD RMF, establishing associated cybersecurity policy, and assigning responsibilities for executing and maintaining the RMF. This DoD policy is consistent with NIST SP 800-37, Guide for Applying the Risk Management Framework, which defines RMF for the Federal Government. CNSSI 1253 and NIST SP 800-53, Security and Privacy Controls for Federal Information Systems and Organizations are incorporated into this DoD policy, which outline the controls and control baselines used in the assessment process. Of critical importance to this SRG, DODI 8510.01 "provides procedural guidance for the reciprocal acceptance of authorization decisions and artifacts within DoD, and between DoD and other federal agencies, for the authorization and connection of information systems (ISs)."

2.4 Federal Risk and Authorization Management Program (FedRAMP)

FedRAMP is a Federal Government program focused on enabling secure cloud computing for the Federal Government. FedRAMP is mandated for use by all Federal Agencies by the Office of Management and Budget (OMB) as their systems and applications are migrated to the commercial cloud under the Federal Government's Cloud-First initiatives. OMB policy requires Federal departments and agencies to utilize FedRAMP approved CSPs and share Agency Authority to Operate (ATO)s with the FedRAMP Secure Repository.

FedRAMP provides a standardized approach to security assessment, authorization, and continuous monitoring for cloud services by incorporating the Federal Government RMF processes. FedRAMP uses a "do once, use many times" framework that intends to reduce cost, time, and staff required for security assessments and process monitoring reports. The FedRAMP Joint Authorization Board (JAB) is the primary governance and decision-making body for the FedRAMP program. JAB approved standards and processes result in the award and maintenance of a Provisional Authorization (PA) to host Federal Government missions.

DoD leverages FedRAMP PAs and U.S. Government Federal Agency ATO packages residing in the FedRAMP Secure Repository, including all supporting documentation.

2.5 FedRAMP Plus (FedRAMP+)

FedRAMP+ is the concept of leveraging the work done as part of the FedRAMP assessment, and adding specific security controls and requirements necessary to meet and assure DoD's critical mission requirements. A CSP's CSO can be assessed in accordance with the criteria outlined in this SRG, with the results used as the basis for awarding a DoD provisional authorization.

2.6 DoD Provisional Authorization

A DoD Provisional Authorization is an acceptance of risk based on an evaluation of the CSPs offering and the potential for risk introduced to DoD networks. It provides a foundation that Authorizing Officials (AOs) responsible for mission applications can leverage in determining the overall risk to the missions/applications that are executed as part of a CSO.

3   INFORMATION SECURITY OBJECTIVES / IMPACT LEVELS

Cloud security information impact levels are defined by the combination of: 1) the level of information to be stored and processed in the CSP environment; and 2) the potential impact of an event that results in the loss of confidentiality, integrity or availability of DoD data, systems or networks. DoD Mission Owners categorize mission information systems in accordance with DoDI 8510.01 and CNSSI 1253 to select the impact level that most closely aligns with defined baselines.

3.1   Security Objectives (Confidentiality, Integrity, Availability)

Information Impact Levels consider the potential impact should the confidentiality or the integrity of the information be compromised.

According to Federal Information Processing Standards (FIPS) Publication 199, *Standards for Security Categorization of Federal Information and Information Systems*, confidentiality is "preserving authorized restrictions on information access and disclosure, including means for protecting personal privacy and proprietary information…" [44 U.S.C., Sec. 3542]. A loss of confidentiality is the unauthorized disclosure of information.

FIPS Publication 199 defines integrity as "Guarding against improper information modification or destruction, and includes ensuring information non-repudiation and authenticity…" [44 U.S.C., Sec. 3542]. A loss of integrity is the unauthorized modification or destruction of information. It is important to note that the unauthorized destruction of information will result in the loss of availability of that information.

FIPS-199 defined three levels to designate the impact of a loss of confidentiality or a loss of integrity (refer to Table 1). The security control baseline for all Impact Levels is based on moderate confidentiality and moderate integrity. If a Mission Owner has high potential impacts, specific requirements must be included in the contract/SLA to address/mitigate this risk or deploy to DoD facilities assessed using CNSSI 1253 high baselines through the DoD RMF. In the future DISA will consider incorporating a FedRAMP High Baseline into this SRG after one becomes available.

Table 1 - Potential Impact Definitions for Security Objectives

Security Objective	Potential Impact		
	Low	**Moderate**	**High**
Confidentiality	The unauthorized disclosure of information could be expected to have a **limited** adverse effect on organizational operations, organizational assets, or individuals.	The unauthorized disclosure of information could be expected to have a **serious** adverse effect on organizational operations, organizational assets, or individuals.	The unauthorized disclosure of information could be expected to have **a severe or catastrophic** adverse effect on organizational operations, organizational assets, or individuals.
Integrity	The unauthorized modification or destruction of information	The unauthorized modification or destruction of information	The unauthorized modification or destruction of information

	could be expected to have a **limited** adverse effect on organizational operations, organizational assets, or individuals.	could be expected to have a **serious** adverse effect on organizational operations, organizational assets, or individuals.	could be expected to have **a severe or catastrophic** adverse effect on organizational operations, organizational assets, or individuals.

The baseline objectives do not address the impact of availability; it is expected that the Mission Owner will assess the CSP's stated availability rating(s) during CSP selection. Any specific or additional availability requirements must be included in the contract or a service level agreement with the CSP. Mission Owners must ensure the language is specific and inclusive for their required availability. For example, if the requirement is "CSP maintenance affecting system availability must be coordinated 4 weeks in advance and only conducted between 02:00 and 04:00 EST on Sunday morning," then the contract / SLA should detail the requirement. Recommended contract / SLA availability controls are provided under the FedRAMP+ Controls/Enhancements in Section 5.1.5, *Controls/Enhancements to be Addressed in the Contract/SLA*.

CSPs will be evaluated or queried as part of the assessment process to determine the level of availability they offer to be listed in the DoD Cloud Service Catalog. This evaluation does not prevent a CSP from receiving a PA or being included in the DoD Cloud Service Catalog; it is only used to facilitate the matching of a DoD Mission Owner to one or more appropriate cloud services meeting their needs.

3.2   Information Impact Levels

The previously published Cloud Security Model defined 6 information Impact Levels. In order to simplify the selection process, the number of levels was reduced from 6 to 4. This was accomplished by integrating levels 1 (public information) and 3 (low impact Controlled Unclassified Information (CUI)) into levels 2 and 4, respectively. The numeric designators for the Impact Levels have not changed to remain consistent with previous versions of the Cloud Security Model, leaving Impact Levels 2, 4, 5, and 6. Note that a higher level can process data from a lower level.

Additionally, the security control baseline for all levels has been changed to moderate confidentiality and moderate integrity as defined by CNSSI 1253 and the FedRAMP Moderate Baseline. This modification from high confidentiality and high integrity is intended to better align with the categorization of most DoD customer systems that will be deployed to commercial CSP facilities. Mission owners with systems categorized at high confidentiality or integrity impact levels must deploy to DoD facilities assessed using CNSSI 1253 high baselines through the DoD RMF or contract for the added security. DISA will consider incorporating a FedRAMP High Baseline into this SRG after one becomes available.

The following subsections describe the impact levels, to include those used previously, and the type of information to be stored or hosted in CSOs.

3.2.1   Level 1: Unclassified Information approved for Public release

Level 1 is no longer used and has been merged with Level 2.

3.2.2 Level 2: Non-Controlled Unclassified Information

Level 2 includes all data cleared for public release, as well as some DoD private unclassified information not designated as CUI or critical mission data, but the information requires some minimal level of access control.

3.2.3 Level 3: Controlled Unclassified Information

Level 3 is no longer used and has been merged with Level 4.

3.2.4 Level 4: Controlled Unclassified Information

Level 4 accommodates CUI which is the categorical designation that refers to unclassified information that under law or policy requires protection from unauthorized disclosure as established by Executive Order 13556 (November 2010) or other mission critical data. Designating information as CUI or critical mission data to be protected at Level 4 is the responsibility of the owning organization. Determination of the appropriate impact level for a specific mission with CUI and mission data will be the responsibility of the mission AO.

CUI contains a number of categories[3], including, but not limited to the following:

- Export Control--Unclassified information concerning certain items, commodities, technology, software, or other information whose export could reasonably be expected to adversely affect the United States national security and nonproliferation objectives. This includes dual use items; items identified in export administration regulations, international traffic in arms regulations and the munitions list; license applications; and sensitive nuclear technology information.
- Privacy Information--Refers to personal information or, in some cases, *personally identifiable information* (PII)[4] as defined in Office of Management and Budget (OMB) M-07-16[5] or *means of identification* as defined in 18 USC 1028(d)(7).
- Protected Health Information (PHI)[6] as defined in the Health Insurance Portability and Accountability Act of 1996 (Public Law 104-191).
- Other information requiring explicit CUI designation (i.e., For Official Use Only, Official Use Only, Law Enforcement Sensitive, Critical Infrastructure Information, and Sensitive Security Information).

3.2.5 Level 5: Controlled Unclassified Information

Level 5 accommodates CUI that requires a higher level of protection as deemed necessary by the information owner, public law, or other government regulations. Level 5 also supports unclassified National Security Systems (NSSs) due to the inclusion of NSS specific requirements in the FedRAMP+ controls/control enhancements (C/CEs). As such, NSS must be implemented at Level 5.

---

[3] CUI Categories: http://www.archives.gov/cui/registry/category-list.html
[4] NIST SP800-22, Protecting PII: http://csrc.nist.gov/publications/nistpubs/800-122/sp800-122.pdf
[5] OMB M-07-16: http://www.whitehouse.gov/sites/default/files/omb/memoranda/fy2007/m07-16.pdf
[6] PHI: http://www.hhs.gov/ocr/privacy/hipaa/understanding/summary/

3.2.6 Level 6: Classified Information up to SECRET

Level 6 accommodates information that has been determined: (i) pursuant to Executive Order 12958 as amended by Executive Order 13292, or any predecessor Order, to be classified national security information; or (ii) pursuant to the Atomic Energy Act of 1954, as amended, to be Restricted Data (RD). At this time, only information classified as SECRET, in accordance with the applicable executive orders, is applicable to this level. Services running at higher classification levels, to include compartmented information, are governed by other policies and are beyond the scope of this document. Impact Level 6 requires a similar set of tailored controls as Level 5 and includes the CNSSI 1253 Appendix F, Attachment 5 Classified Information Overlay C/CEs.

UNCLASSIFIED

4 RISK ASSESSMENT OF CLOUD SERVICE OFFERINGS

The shift to cloud computing necessitates changes in the Risk Management processes. The goal is to address the security requirements and controls, relative to the criticality of DoD information in the external cloud, in a cost effective and efficient manner, while still assuring the security of DoD's core missions and networks in accordance with the DoD RMF. To support the relationship of missions to cloud capabilities, DoD has defined information Impact Levels (discussed in Section 3) that broadly align to the criticality, sensitivity of data, and missions that would operate in a cloud environment. The DoD provisional authorization (PA) risk assessment process is focused on evaluating the requirements for the impact level(s) at which a CSP's Cloud Service Offering (CSO) is capable of supporting. The resulting PA would then be leveraged by the Mission Owner's Authorization Official in granting an authorization to operate (ATO) for the mission system operating within the cloud.

4.1 Assessment of Commercial/Non-DoD Cloud Services

The 15 December 2014 DoD CIO memo regarding *Updated Guidance on the Acquisition and Use of Commercial Cloud Computing Services,* states "components may host Unclassified DoD information that **has been publicly released** on FedRAMP approved cloud services." The memo also states "FedRAMP will serve as the minimum security baseline for all DoD cloud services."

Impact Level 2: Using the definitions outlined in section 3, Impact Level 2 information may be hosted in a CSP that is government assessed as FedRAMP compliant at the moderate level. The two acceptable government assessments include:

- JAB Provisional Authorizations – Based on a determination by the JAB that an acceptable level of risk exists for leveraging across the Federal Government. DoD is an active participant in the technical reviews of the JAB PA security assessment artifacts.
- Agency ATOs – Based on an assessment and ATO issued by a specific agency. These are assessed and authorized by a DoD agency, with the artifacts made available for leveraging by others across the Federal Government.

The decision to leverage such authorizations is subject to acceptance by the Mission Owner and the responsible Authorizing Official (AO).

Impact Level 4/5/6: Assessments for Impact Levels 4 and above is based on a combination of the security controls in the FedRAMP Moderate baseline and the DoD specific controls/requirements outlined in section 5.1.2 DoD FedRAMP+ Controls/Enhancements. Where possible, DoD leverages documentation and artifacts in the FedRAMP Secure Repository and additional CSP proprietary artifacts. FedRAMP+ requirements will be assessed by a FedRAMP certified Third Party Assessment Organization (3PAO) or an approved DoD assessor. An overall determination of risk is prepared by the DISA Cloud Security Control Assessors to support a DoD PA decision and listing in the DoD Cloud Service Catalog[7], available to DoD personnel. The DISA Authorizing Official (AO) (formerly the DISA DAA) approves DoD PAs.

There are three paths that can be followed in assessing a CSP for a DoD PA. These are:

---

[7] DoD Cloud Service Catalog:
https://disa.deps.mil/disa/org/atb/Cloud%20Broker/Lists/Catalog/CatalogPageView.aspx (DoD PKI required)

- **CSPs with a FedRAMP JAB PA or in the process of obtaining a JAB PA:** DoD leverages the documentation and artifacts produced as part of the FedRAMP process, supplemented with an assessment of the DoD-specific security controls and requirements not addressed by FedRAMP for Impact Levels 4 and above. CSPs having a FedRAMP JAB PA have been assessed by a certified 3PAO against the FedRAMP Moderate Baseline. For those in the process of obtaining a JAB PA, DoD promotes the use of parallel activities (FedRAMP and FedRAMP+) to minimize cost and create efficiencies in the assessment process.

- **FedRAMP Agency ATO:** CSPs having a Federal agency authorization based upon security controls assessed by a certified 3PAO can be assessed for a DoD PA provided that the authorization is accepted and listed in the FedRAMP agency authorizations. The information from the agency ATO will be supplemented with an assessment of the DoD-specific controls and requirements.

- **DoD Self-Assessed PA:** CSP is assessed by the DISA cloud assessment team, independent of FedRAMP. The CSP is minimally assessed against the FedRAMP Moderate Baseline and FedRAMP+ requirements. A DoD self-assessment is typically used for dedicated cloud service offerings supporting the DoD or a private cloud service offering by a DoD or commercial CSP. In this scenario, the CSP's assessment package will not be in the FedRAMP secure repository, since private clouds are ineligible for inclusion in the FedRAMP catalog. When a FedRAMP authorization does not exist for a commercial CSP, the DoD organization with a need for the authorization will be required to support resourcing for the full assessment, in coordination with the DISA cloud security assessment team. This assessment of both the FedRAMP, FedRAMP+ security controls, and other SRG requirements determines whether to grant a DoD PA and the appropriate impact levels.

NOTE: Any change of ownership involving a CSP, whether the primary CSP or an underlying CSP on which a CSO was built, will be reviewed by the DISA AO to assess the impacts and risks associated with the continuation of the DoD PA.

4.2   Assessment of DoD Provided Cloud Services

DoD operated CSOs (e.g., milCloud) are subject to the same requirements found in this SRG and the same security controls as commercial CSPs. However, DoD CSP programs and services must follow DoD Risk Management procedures in accordance with DoDI 8510.01. DoD enterprise service programs considered as cloud services under the SaaS model (e.g., Defense Enterprise Email (DEE), Defense Connect Online (DCO), DoD Enterprise Portal Service (DEPS)), are also subject to the DoDI 8510.01 requirements. Such programs are not subject to being assessed through the FedRAMP program and do not share DoD ATOs with the FedRAMP secure repository.

DoD is transitioning to the DoD RMF from the DoD Information Assurance Certification and Accreditation Process (DIACAP). DIACAP is based on a set of DoD specific security controls, not the NIST 800-53 security control catalog. Cloud services initiated and authorized under the

DIACAP will be assessed and authorized using the RMF in accordance with DoD transition guidance as defined in DODI 8510.01 or supplemental DoD guidance.

4.3 Cloud Service Offering and Mission Owner Risk Management

Risk management must consider both the CSO and the supported mission (i.e., the Mission Owner's system or application). Each CSO must be granted a DoD PA in order to host DoD mission systems. The PA can then be used by the Mission Owner's risk management officials as a basis of reciprocity for the controls provided by the CSP, recognizing the controls will vary based on the service model (IaaS, PaaS, SaaS) and could also vary based on requirements such as privacy or classification controls. Additionally, there are controls that are "shared controls" where both the CSO and the Mission Owner need to address a requirement. The responsible AO leverages the PA information, supplemented with an assessment of the risks within the Mission Owner's responsibility, in granting an authorization to operate.

Understanding the distinction between what's provided and addressed with the CSO versus what's addressed by the Mission Owner is critical to implementing the DoD cloud security requirements as defined in this SRG.

4.3.1 Cloud Service Offering (CSO) Risk

The DoD PA provides a risk acceptance determination for the CSO against the appropriate DoD security requirements. The DoD PA assessment process assesses CSO risk based on its supported impact level. At a level 4 and above, it's important to recognize that the DoD PA evaluation process also assesses the risk to DoD of permitting CSPs to interconnect with DoD networks.

4.3.2 Mission Risk

Overall mission risk will continue to be assessed and authorized by the Mission Owner's AO through the issuance of an ATO. Mission refers to the information system and functions for which a DoD entity acquires or uses a CSO. This may be the direct use of a SaaS CSO in performing an IT-enabled mission, or the instantiation of an IT system or application on an IaaS/PaaS CSO.

Mission Owners categorize mission systems and/or applications in accordance with (IAW) DoDI 8510.01 defined processes. Mission owners then select CSOs from the DoD Cloud Service Catalog based on their security posture and the risk tolerance of the Mission Owner. While CSOs will have been assessed and provisionally authorized for use, the Mission Owner must proceed IAW the RMF to obtain an Authority To Operate (ATO) from their assigned AO.

The Mission Owner inherits compliance from the CSO for the security controls (or portions thereof) that the CSP meets and maintains. A Mission Owner's system or application built on an IaaS or PaaS offering will be subject to meeting many of the same security controls within the system/application. Mission Owners contracting for SaaS offerings inherit the bulk of compliance with the security controls from the CSO. Inheritance will be different between CSPs operating within a service type and thus must be evaluated separately. It should also be noted that the number of controls increases with higher impact levels and additional overlay controls (e.g. privacy). Figure 1 illustrates this concept.

UNCLASSIFIED

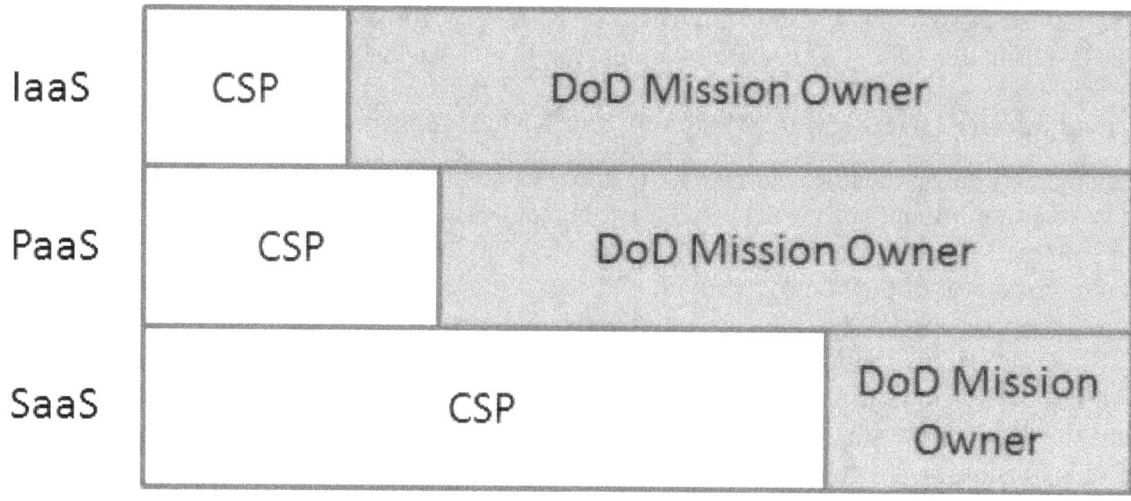

Security Responsibility

Figure 1 – Notional Division of Security Inheritance and Risk

The benefit of starting with a provisionally authorized CSO is that much of the security controls assessment work is already accomplished. Mission Owners and their AOs must still review the FedRAMP and DoD PA artifacts to understand the risks that the mission will inherit when using the selected CSO for the mission system/application. Mission owners may need to implement, or request that the CSP implement, compensating controls for any risk deemed unacceptable prior to obtaining an ATO.

4.4 CSP Transition from CSM v2.1 to SRG v1r1

FedRAMP provides a transition strategy[8] for migrating CSP assessments from the FedRAMP v1 baselines based on NIST 800-53 rev3 to the FedRAMP v2 baselines based on NIST 800-53 rev4. This strategy went into effect on June 6, 2014. The key points are as follows:

- Any new assessment starting after June 1, 2014 will immediately transition to FedRAMP v2 baselines based on NIST 800-53 rev4.
- CSPs in the process of being assessed against FedRAMP v1 baselines based on NIST 800-53 rev3 prior to June 1, 2014 will continue on this track, but must transition to the FedRAMP v2 baselines within one year of their authorization date.
- CSPs currently in continuous monitoring will have until their next annual assessment to complete the transition to FedRAMP v2 baselines.

The requirements in this SRG become effective immediately upon final publication. However, the DoD migration plan for CSP assessments will mirror the FedRAMP plan as follows:

- Any new assessment starting after the release of this Cloud Computing SRG will be assessed against these requirements.

---

[8] FedRAMP transition strategy: http://cloud.cio.gov/topics/fedramp-800-53-rev-4-guidance-cloud-service-providers-0

UNCLASSIFIED

- CSPs currently in the process of being assessed against the requirements in the CSMv2.1 will continue on this track, but must transition to compliance with the Cloud Computing SRG requirements in coordination with their next FedRAMP annual assessment.
- CSPs currently in continuous monitoring under CSMv2.1 will have until their next FedRAMP annual assessment to complete the transition to compliance with the Cloud Computing SRG control requirements.

A DoD PA issued for a CSP using the CSMv2.1 and based on FedRAMP v1 remains in effect for the duration of the DoD PA, so long as compliance is achieved with the timelines described above. DoD mission systems leveraging a CSO may experience a period of time of time where risks based on FedRAMP v2 or new FedRAMP+ security controls have not yet been assessed. Mission owners and their AOs must review the controls to determine if the risk is acceptable until such time the CSP is required to comply or include the required compliance in the acquisition language.

NOTE: CSPs wishing to transition sooner than later may do so at any time.

This page is intentionally blank.

5 SECURITY REQUIREMENTS

This section of the SRG defines the security requirements for DoD's use of cloud computing. It covers several areas as follows:

- Security requirements for CSP's service offerings.
- Security requirements for assessing commercial and DoD CSPs for inclusion in the DoD Cloud Service Catalog.Security requirements for Mission Owner's systems/applications instantiated on IaaS/PaaS.

5.1 DoD Policy Regarding Security Controls

DoDI 8500.01 requires all DoD Information Systems to be categorized in accordance with CNSSI 1253 and implement a corresponding set of security controls and control enhancements (C/CEs) that are published in NIST SP 800-53, regardless of whether they are National Security Systems (NSS) or non-NSS.

The CNSSI 1253 baselines are tailored from the NIST 800-53 recommended baselines, as are the FedRAMP baselines. These baselines are a starting point for securing all DoD systems, which can be tailored further to address specific systems and situations.

See NIST SP 800-59, *Guideline for Identifying an Information System as a National Security System,*[9] for a definition of NSS and further information.

5.1.1 DoD use of FedRAMP Security Controls

The FedRAMP Low and Moderate baselines are a tailored set of C/CEs based on the Low and Moderate baselines recommended in NIST SP 800-53 catalog of security controls.

The 15 December 2014 DoD CIO memo regarding *Updated Guidance on the Acquisition and Use of Commercial Cloud Computing Services* states "FedRAMP will serve as the minimum security baseline for all DoD cloud services." This SRG uses the FedRAMP v2 Moderate baseline at all information impact levels.

The 2014 DoD CIO memo further states "components may host Unclassified DoD information that has been publicly released on FedRAMP approved cloud services". Using the definitions defined in section 3, Impact Level 2 information may be hosted in a CSP that minimally holds a FedRAMP Moderate PA (with or without a DoD PA); subject to compliance with the personnel security requirements outlined in section 5.6.2 and acceptance by the Mission Owner and the responsible Authorizing Official (AO). The FedRAMP v2 Moderate baseline, supplemented with DoD FedRAMP+ C/CEs and requirements in this SRG, are used to assess CSPs toward awarding a DoD PA at information impact levels 4 and above.

5.1.2 DoD FedRAMP+ Security Controls/Enhancements

A tailored baseline of security C/CEs has been developed for each DoD information impact level, except for level 2. These baselines incorporate, but are not limited to, the FedRAMP Moderate baseline. The DoD cloud baseline C/CEs, which are beyond what is required by FedRAMP (otherwise referred to as FedRAMP+ C/CEs), were selected primarily because they

---

[9] NIST SP 800-59: http://csrc.nist.gov/publications/PubsSPs.html

address issues such as the Advanced Persistent Threat (APT) and/or Insider Threat, and because the DoD, unlike the rest of the Federal Government, must categorize its systems in accordance with CNSSI 1253.

The CNSSI 1253 baseline used in support of DoD PAs is based on Moderate Confidentiality and Moderate Integrity, not including a baseline for Availability (categorization designated as M-M-x). Availability is to be addressed by the Mission Owner in the contract/SLA. The resulting M-M-x baseline was compared to the FedRAMP Moderate baseline to derive a tailored set of FedRAMP+ security controls/enhancements for each level. Based on this comparison, we find that the FedRAMP Moderate Baseline includes approximately thirty two (32) C/CEs that are also contained in the CNSSI 1253 M-M-x baseline, but not in the NIST 800-35 Moderate baseline incorporated in both. We also find that eighty eight (88) of the C/CEs are not in the FedRAMP baseline. These 88 were analyzed for their benefit and projected cost and approximately half were selected for the DoD cloud baselines. The number of control enhancements selected varies by impact level.

Although the control baselines for all levels are based on those from CNSSI 1253, only impact Level 5 and 6 are designed to accommodate NSS. NSS-specific Cs/CEs have been included at these levels along with those required for the higher impact of these levels. Thus, an unclassified NSS must be instantiated at level 5. This, however, does not preclude an unclassified non-NSS from operating at Level 5 if the mission requires the added security. Since Impact Level 6 is for classified NSS, it is also subject to the CNSSI 1253 Classified Overlay which imposes ninety eight (98) additional controls/enhancements. For IaaS/PaaS service offerings, there may only be a portion of the classified overlay applicable to the CSP with the balance of the controls/enhancements being fulfilled by the Mission Owner. This division of responsibility will be addressed in a future release of this document or in a companion document.

Additionally, any level that deals with PII or PHI is additionally subject to the CNSSI 1253 Privacy Overlay (when published). This overlay adds most of the privacy specific C/CEs from NIST SP 800-53 rev4 Appendix J Privacy Control Catalog and provides additional supplemental guidance for many of the selected C/CEs in other families. It was developed in accordance with Privacy Act and HIPAA requirements, leveraging experts and lawyers in both fields. Legal references are included as the basis for C/CE selection and supplemental guidance. This overlay is fully applicable to CSP's SaaS offerings that handle PII/PHI with some C/CEs (e.g., the required System of Records Notice in accordance with TR-2) being addressed by the Mission Owner. For IaaS/PaaS offerings, only a portion of the overlay may be applicable to the CSP with most C/CEs being fulfilled by the Mission Owner. This in no way alleviates any requirement incumbent upon the CSP for protecting privacy act information related to its customers and their accounts.

Table 2 provides a listing of the FedRAMP+ C/CEs applicable to each information impact level, which includes only one additional base control. The rest are control enhancements. This table does not include controls added by the Classified Information or Privacy overlays. These additional FedRAMP+ and overlay Cs/CEs must be implemented and documented by the CSP.

NOTE: This table does not include the FedRAMP Moderate baseline[10] C/CEs, a table of which can be obtained from the FedRAMP website[11] on the Templates and Key Documents page[12].

Table 2 - DoD FedRAMP+ Security Controls/Enhancements

SP 800-53r4 Cont./Enh. ID	Level 4	Level 5	Level 6
AC-06 (07)	X	X	X
AC-06 (08)	X	X	X
AC-17 (06)	X	X	X
AC-18 (03)	X	X	X
AC-23	X	X	X
AT-03 (02)	X	X	X
AT-03 (04)	X	X	X
AU-04 (01)	X	X	X
AU-06 (04)	X	X	X
AU-06 (10)	X	X	X
AU-12 (01)	X	X	X
CA-03 (01)		X	n/a
CM-03 (04)	X	X	X
CM-03 (06)	X	X	X
CM-04 (01)	X	X	X
CM-05 (06)	X	X	X
IA-02 (09)	X	X	X
IA-05 (13)	X	X	X
IR-04 (03)	X	X	X
IR-04 (04)	X	X	X
IR-04 (06)	X	X	X

---

[10] FedRAMP Security Controls: http://cloud.cio.gov/document/fedramp-security-controls
[11] FedRAMP website: http://cloud.cio.gov/fedramp
[12] FedRAMP Templates and Key Documents: http://cloud.cio.gov/fedramp/templates

UNCLASSIFIED

IR-04 (07)	X	X	X
IR-04 (08)	X	X	X
IR-06 (02)	X	X	X
MA-04 (03)	X	X	X
MA-04 (06)	X	X	X
PE-03 (01)	X	X	X
PL-08 (01)		X	X
PS-04 (01)		X	X
PS-06 (03)		X	X
SA-04 (07)		X	X
SC-07 (10)	X	X	X
SC-07 (11)		X	X
SC-07 (14)			X
SC-08 (02)		X	X
SC-23 (01)	X	X	X
SC-23 (03)	X	X	X
SC-23 (05)		X	X
SI-02 (06)	X	X	X
SI-03 (10)		X	X
SI-04 (12)	X	X	X
SI-04 (19)	X	X	X
SI-04 (20)	X	X	X
SI-04 (22)	X	X	X
SI-10 (03)	X	X	X
Total	35 PLUS Privacy Overlay if required	44 PLUS Privacy Overlay if required	44 PLUS 98 from Classified Overlay

UNCLASSIFIED

NOTE: CSPs may offer equivalent controls or mitigations which will be considered on a case-by-case basis.

5.1.3 Parameter Values for Security Controls and Enhancements

Many NIST SP 800-53 Security Controls and enhancements contain parameter values that are left, by NIST, to the organization to define. For those controls required by FedRAMP and the DoD, the parameter values are defined in Appendix D.

5.1.4 Security Controls/Enhancements to be Addressed in the Contract/SLA

Table 3 shows the C/CEs designated for the Mission Owner to optionally address in the contract or SLA, over and above the FedRAMP and FedRAMP+ C/CEs which must be included by default. While these C/CEs generally address system availability, they apply to the availability of information related to continuous monitoring, incident response, and other security issues. It must be noted that this listing does not preclude the Mission Owner from addressing any control or enhancement from any CNSSI 1253 baseline or the NIST SP 800-53 rev4 in the contract/SLA if they need the control/enhancement to be provided/met by the CSP to secure their system or application. Assessment and continuous monitoring of compliance with these C/CEs is the responsibility of the Mission Owner as negotiated with the CSP in attaining and maintaining the mission's ATO. These C/CEs are not assessed toward the award of a DoD PA.

Table 3 - Security Controls/Enhancements to be addressed in the contract/SLA

SP 800-53r4 Cont./Enh. ID	Level 4	Level 5	Level 6
AC-02 (13)	X	X	X
AC-03 (04)	X	X	X
AC-12 (01)		X	X
AC-16	X	X	X
AC-16 (06)	X	X	X
AU-10		X	X
IA-03 (01)	X	X	X
PS-04 (01)	X		
PS-06 (03)	X		
SA-12		X	X
SA-19		X	X
SC-07 (11)	X		

SC-07 (14)	X	X	
SC-18 (03)		X	X
SC-18 (04)		X	X
Total	9	12	11

5.2 Legal Considerations

5.2.1 Jurisdiction/Location Requirements

Legal considerations, including legal jurisdiction, control where DoD and US government data can be located.

Impact Level 2/4: CSPs will maintain all government data that is not physically located on DoD premises within the 50 States, the District of Columbia, and outlying areas of the US. Authorizing Officials (AO), after careful consideration of the legal ramifications, may authorize other locations if necessary to support mission requirements. Information regarding AO authorized processing locations will be provided to the supporting CND providers and DISA's cloud services support office.

Impact Level 5/6: To protect against seizure and improper use by non-US persons and government entities, all data / information stored and processed for the DoD must reside in a facility under the exclusive legal jurisdiction of the US. CSPs will maintain all government data that is not physically located on DoD premises within the 50 States, the District of Columbia, and outlying areas of the US.

DoD CSPs will, and commercial CSPs may (under DoD contract), instantiate their cloud service architecture on DoD premises (DoD on-premises). Interconnection with DoD networks will be interoperable IAW engineering requirements that meet cybersecurity guidance and controls. DoD on-premises includes DoD data centers, other facilities located on a DoD B/C/P/S, or in a commercial or another government facility (or portions thereof) under the direct control of DoD personnel and DoD security policies. A commercial facility in this sense means a building or space leased and controlled by DoD. Physical facilities may be permanent buildings or portable structures such as transit/shipping containers. An example of the latter might be a container housing a commercial CSP's infrastructure located adjacent to a Core Data Center (CDC) and connected to its network as if it was inside the building. A CSP will provide the agency a list of the physical locations where the data could be stored at any given time and update that list as new physical locations are added.

5.2.2 Cloud Deployment Model Considerations / Separation Requirements

The risks and legal considerations in using virtualization technologies further restrict the types of tenants that can obtain cloud services from a virtualized environment on the same physical infrastructure and the types of cloud deployment models (i.e., public, private, community, and hybrid) in which the various types of DoD information may be processed or stored.

While shared cloud environments provide significant opportunities for DoD entities, they also present unique risks to DoD data and systems that must be addressed. These risks include exploitation of vulnerabilities in virtualization technologies, interfaces to external systems, APIs, and management systems. These have the potential for providing back door connections and CSP privileged user access to customer's systems and data (insider threat). While proper configuration of the virtual and physical environment can mitigate many of these threats, there is still residual risk that may or may not be acceptable to DoD. Legal concerns such as e-discovery and law enforcement seizure of non-government CSP customer/tenant's data pose a threat to DoD data if it is in the same storage media. Due to these concerns, DoD is currently taking a cautious approach with regard to Level 5 information.

Infrastructure (as related to cloud services), is the physical hardware (i.e., server platforms and storage), and the network interconnecting the hardware that supports the cloud service and its virtualization technology (if used). This includes the systems and networks used by the CSP to manage the infrastructure. While the physical space in which this infrastructure is housed is part of the CSP's infrastructure, this is not a factor in DoD's restrictions except at Level 6.

Dedicated infrastructure (as related to cloud services) refers to the cloud service infrastructure being dedicated to serving a single customer organization or a specific group of customer organizations. A private cloud service implements dedicated infrastructure to serve one customer organization. A community cloud service implements dedicated infrastructure to serve a specific group or class of customer organizations. Both can serve multiple tenants (missions) within the customer organizations the service supports.

Shared infrastructure, for the purpose of this SRG, refers to the physical cloud infrastructure being available to DoD and Federal Government tenants as well as non-DoD and Non-Federal Government tenants. This is also referred to as a public cloud.

It is important to note that while clouds marketed as "International Traffic in Arms (ITAR) compliant,", "government clouds,", or "clouds for government" might restrict data location to US jurisdiction, they do not necessarily meet the standard for "dedicated" for the Federal Government or DoD. If the cloud service, or the underlying infrastructure it resides on, contains any non-Federal US government tenant such as state or local governments, industry partners, or foreign governments, it is a considered shared infrastructure for purposes of this SRG.

NOTE: The use of the term "ITAR compliant" in a CSP's marketing documentation may or may not mean that the Department of State's Directorate of Defense Trade Controls or the Department of Commerce's Bureau of Industry and Services certified and documented the service offering as truly ITAR compliant. The CSP must substantiate their claim by providing access to valid documentation or the DoD Mission Owner must validate such claims before the Mission Owner considers the service offering based on its advertised compliance.

5.2.2.1 Impact Levels 2 and 4 Location and Separation Requirements

Impact Level 2 cloud services can be offered on either shared or dedicated infrastructure. Information that may be processed and stored at Impact Levels 2 and 4 can be processed on-premises or off-premises in any cloud deployment model that restricts the physical location of the information as described in section 5.2.1, "Jurisdiction/Location Requirements."

Information that may be processed and stored at Impact Level 4 can be offered on either shared or dedicated infrastructure. Information that can be processed and stored at Impact Level 4 can be processed on-premises or off-premises in any cloud deployment model that restricts the physical location of the information as described in section 5.2.1, "Jurisdiction/Location Requirements."

The CSP must provide evidence of strong virtual separation controls and monitoring, and the ability to meet "search and seizure" requests without the release of DoD information and data.

5.2.2.2 Impact Level 5 Location and Separation Requirements

Information that must be processed and stored at Impact Level 5 can only be processed in a dedicated infrastructure, on-premises or off-premises in any cloud deployment model that restricts the physical location of the information as described in section 5.2.1, "Jurisdiction/Location Requirements." This excludes public service offerings.

The following applies:

- Only DoD private, DoD community or Federal Government community clouds are eligible for Impact Level 5.
- Each deployment model may support multiple missions or tenants / missions from each customer organization.
- Virtual/logical separation between DoD and Federal Government tenants / missions is permitted.
- Virtual/logical separation between tenant/mission systems is minimally required.
- Physical separation (e.g. Dedicated Infrastructure) from non-DoD/non-Federal Government tenants is required.

NOTE: A CSP may offer alternate solutions that provide equivalent security to the stated requirements. Approval will be assessed on a case by case basis during the PA assessment process.

5.2.2.3 Impact Level 6 Location and Separation Requirements

Impact Level 6 is reserved for the storage and processing of classified information. The following applies:

- Impact Level 6 information up to the SECRET level must be stored and processed in a dedicated cloud infrastructure located in facilities approved for the processing of classified information, rated at or above the highest level of classification of the information being stored and/or processed.
- On-premises locations are approved through DoD processes and are operated in accordance with DoD and Director of National Intelligence (DNI) policies.
- Off-premises locations that restrict the physical location of the information as described in section 5.2.1, "Jurisdiction/Location Requirements" are approved in accordance with the National Industrial Security Program (NISP) as defined in Executive Order 12829 and the National Industrial Security Program Operating Manual (NISPOM)[13], DoD 5220.22-M.
- A Facility Security Clearance[14] and cleared personnel are required.
- The hosting organization must operate the facility in accordance with the NISPOM.

---

[13] NISPOM: http://www.dss.mil/documents/odaa/nispom2006-5220.pdf
[14] DSS Facility Clearance Branch: http://www.dss.mil/isp/fac_clear/fac_clear.html

- Only DoD private, DoD community or Federal Government community clouds which are stand-alone or connected to SECRET networks (e.g., SIPRNet) are eligible for Impact Level 6.
- Each deployment model may support multiple SECRET missions from each customer organization.
- Virtual/logical separation between DoD and Federal Government tenants / SECRET missions is permitted.
- Virtual/logical separation between tenant/mission systems is minimally required.
- Physical separation (e.g. Dedicated Infrastructure) from non-DoD/non-Federal Government tenants is required.

5.3   Ongoing Assessment

Both FedRAMP and DoD requires an ongoing assessment and authorization capability for CSPs providing services to the DoD. This capability is built upon the DoD RMF and the foundation of the FedRAMP continuous monitoring strategy, as described in the FedRAMP CONOPS and Continuous Monitoring Strategy Guide. These ongoing assessment processes which are discussed in the following sections include continuous monitoring and change control.

5.3.1   Continuous Monitoring

CSPs, 3PAOs, and DoD assessors are responsible for providing deliverables attesting to the implementation of security controls. Continuous monitoring data flows will differ for CSPs depending on whether they have a FedRAMP JAB PA, a 3PAO assessed Federal Agency ATO, or DoD Self-Assessed PA (as described in Section 4). These data flows are reflected in Figure 2, Figure 3, and Figure 4 respectively.

In some cases, CSPs will provide continuous monitoring artifacts directly to DISA. In such cases, the CSP will utilize commercial standard formats (e.g., comma-separated values, XML) that enable DoD to automate the ingest of continuous monitoring data.

This section pertains specifically to continuous monitoring of security controls, as defined by CNSSI 4009 and NIST SP800-137. This is separate from monitoring activities performed as part of Computer Network Defense, which are described in Section 6.

5.3.1.1   CSPs in the FedRAMP Catalog

As described in section 4.1 Assessment of Commercial/Non-DoD Cloud Services, the CSPs, acceptable to DoD in the FedRAMP catalog include CSPs having a JAB PA (which is 3PAO assessed) or a 3PAO assessed Federal Agency ATO. These CSPs will provide all reports required by the FedRAMP Continuous Monitoring Strategy Guide, including self- assessments, to the FedRAMP Information System Security Officer (ISSO). These will be reviewed by the FedRAMP TRs and approved by the JAB if necessary.

Continuous monitoring requirements for DoD are the same as those for FedRAMP, except that all reports and artifacts for FedRAMP+ C/CEs will be provided directly to DISA AO representatives as the DoD single point of CSP contact for this information. DISA will share all continuous monitoring information (FedRAMP and FedRAMP+) with appropriate Mission Owners, AOs, and Computer Network Defense (CND) Service Providers (CNDSPs).

The information will be used by Mission Owners, their AOs, and the DISA AO to evaluate the risk posture of the CSP's services. Those evaluations will inform decisions to continue the ATO for the Mission Owner's system and the PA for the CSP respectively. The DISA AO will coordinate closely with Mission Owners in the event that the withdrawal of a PA must be considered upon the basis of this requirement.

Figure 2 shows the normal flow of continuous monitoring information if the CSP has a FedRAMP JAB PA.

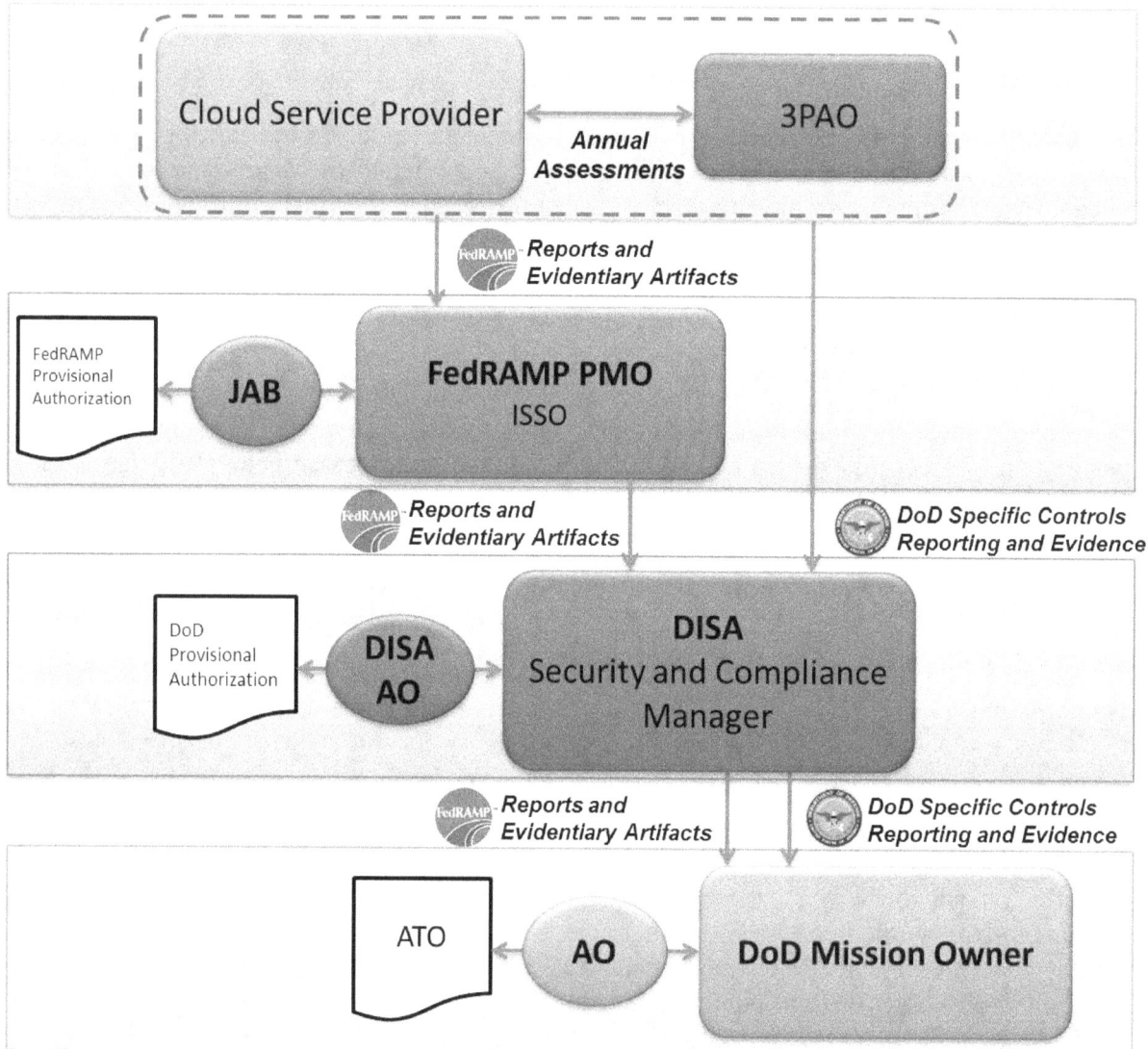

Figure 2 – DoD Continuous Monitoring for CSPs with a FedRAMP JAB PA

Figure 3 shows the flow of continuous monitoring information if the CSP has a 3PAO assessed Federal Agency ATO listed in the FedRAMP catalog. Since the FedRAMP JAB does not control the Agency ATO, information may not flow from the CSP to the FedRAMP PMO.

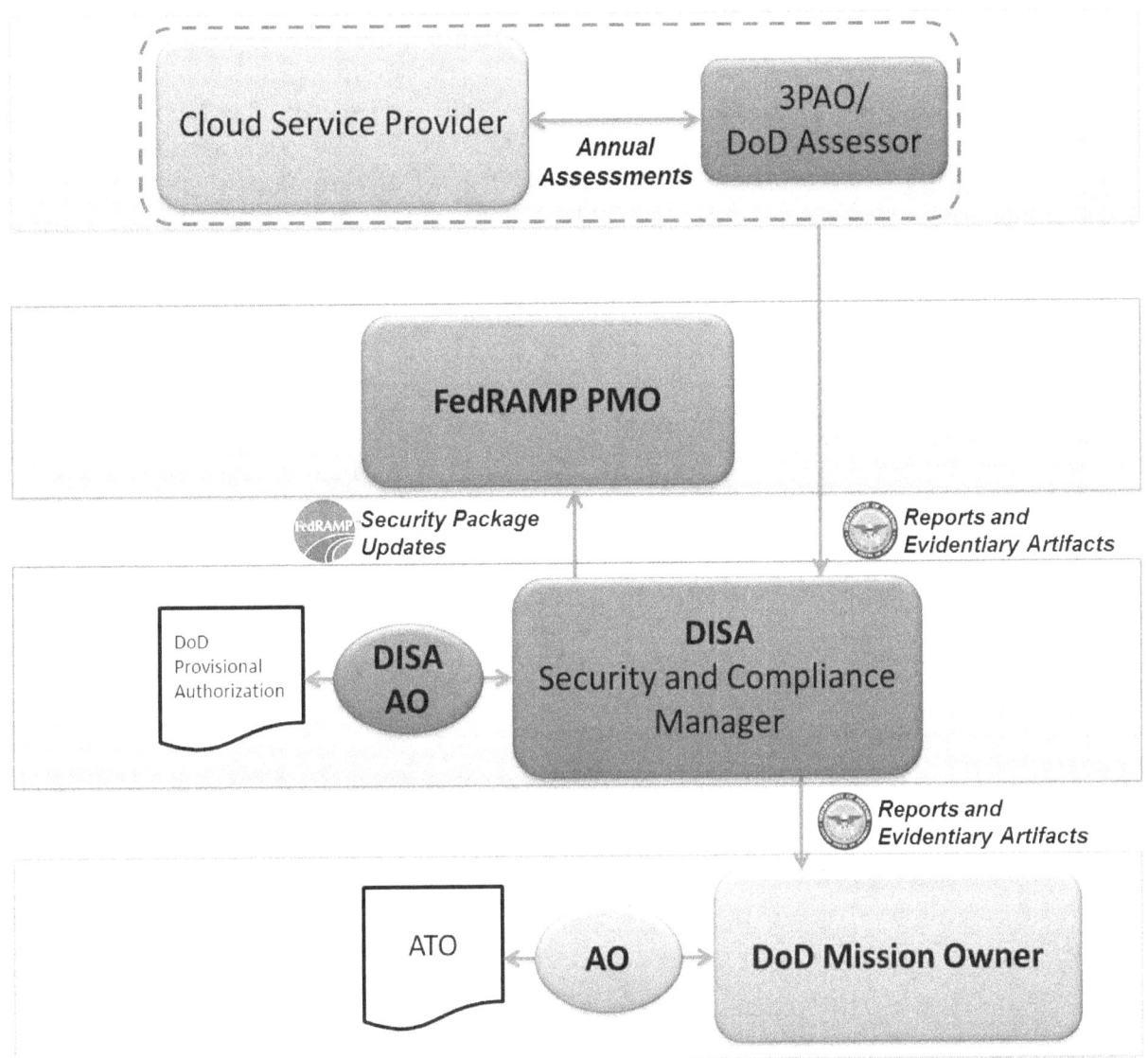

Figure 3 – DoD Continuous Monitoring for FedRAMP CSPs with a 3PAO assessed Federal Agency ATO

5.3.1.2 DoD Self-Assessed CSPs

Figure 4 shows the flow of continuous monitoring information for non-FedRAMP CSPs having a DoD PA or ATO. Continuous monitoring will be directed by the DoD RMF, rather than the FedRAMP Continuous Monitoring Strategy Guide. As part of the RMF authorization process, CSPs will create a continuous monitoring strategy that meets DoD requirements in the System Security Plan. All reports and artifacts required by that continuous monitoring strategy will be provided by the CSP to DISA. DISA will, in turn, disseminate those artifacts to all Mission Owners utilizing that CSO, the DISA AO, and the Computer Network Defense Service Provider (CNDSP) entities as defined in section 6, "Computer Network Defense and Incident Response."

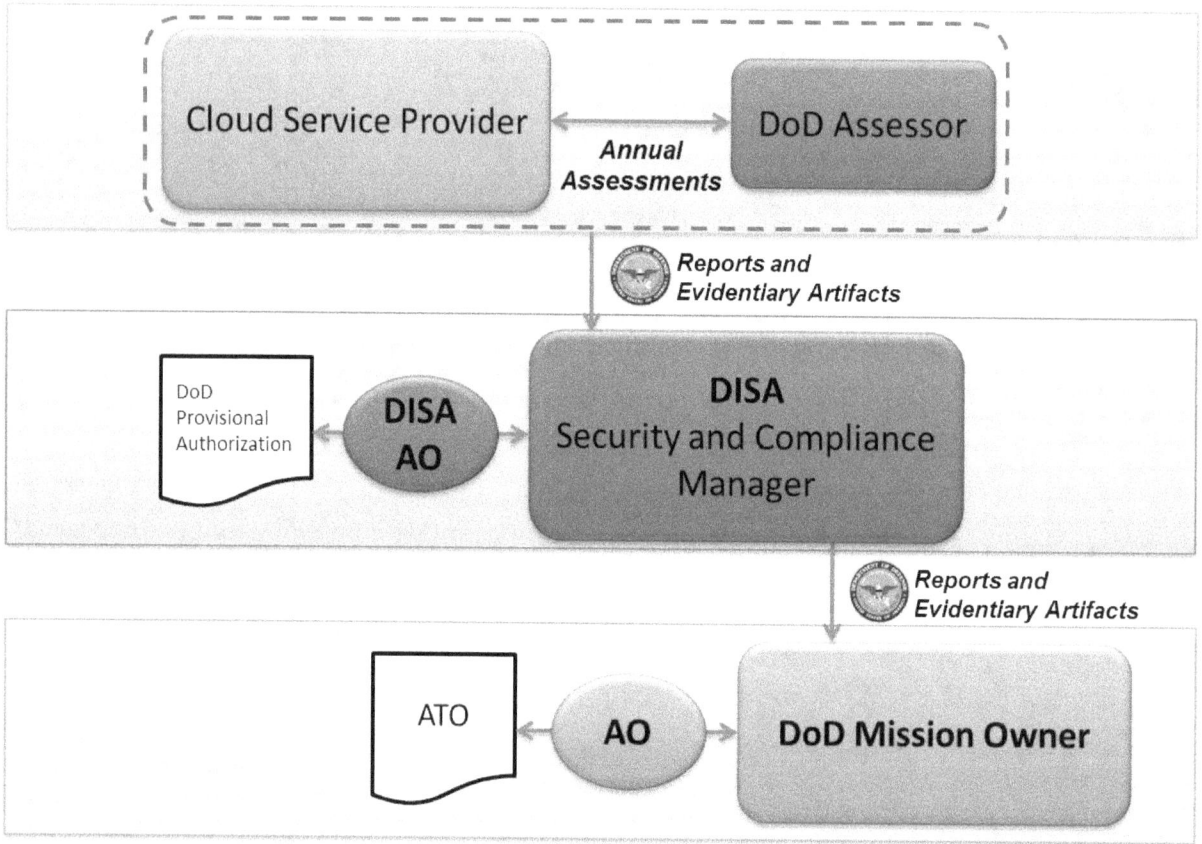

Figure 4 – DoD Continuous Monitoring for DoD Self-Assessed CSPs

5.3.2 Change Control

The DoD will review all significant changes planned by a CSP. Like continuous monitoring, the change control process will differ for CSPs depending on if they are in the FedRAMP catalog and if they have a DoD assessed PA or AO. Figure 5, Figure 6, and Figure 7 show these change control processes.

5.3.2.1 CSPs in the FedRAMP Catalog

FedRAMP defines a significant change as a change to the scope of an approved PA or an impact to the authorization boundary of the CSO. The FedRAMP *Significant Change Security Impact Analysis Form* enumerates significant changes. The review of significant changes will be performed at multiple layers, as reflected in Figure 5. As part of the FedRAMP process, when the CSP holds a FedRAMP PA, the CSP will notify the FedRAMP ISSO of any planned significant change and subsequently provide a Security Impact Analysis for the planned change. The planned change will be reviewed by the ISSO and/or JAB Technical Representatives (TRs), and then forwarded to the JAB for approval. During ISSO review, the DoD JAB TR will inform the FedRAMP ISSO if planned changes will adversely affect the security of the information hosted by the CSP for DoD cloud customers. The DoD JAB TR will notify DISA, who will in turn notify all Mission Owners utilizing that CSO, the DISA AO, and the CNDSP entities as defined in section 6, "Computer Network Defense and Incident Response."

When a CSP is included in the FedRAMP catalog, but does not have a JAB PA, the CSP will notify DISA directly, who will in turn notify the all Mission Owners utilizing that CSO, the DISA AO, and the CNDSP entities as defined in section 6, "Computer Network Defense and Incident Response." For CSPs in the DoD Cloud Service Catalog, the Security Impact Analysis must additionally cover the FedRAMP+ C/CEs. Once informed, DISA will review the proposed change to assess if it will, and ensure it will not, adversely affect the security of the DoD Information Network (DoDIN) with respect to the impact level at which it is authorized. The planned change will also be reviewed by the Mission Owners consuming the CSP's services for any adverse impact with regard to their specific usage of the CSO. Any updates to the FedRAMP Security Package will be forwarded to DISA.

UNCLASSIFIED

Figure 5 shows the normal flow of significant change information if the CSP has a FedRAMP JAB PA.

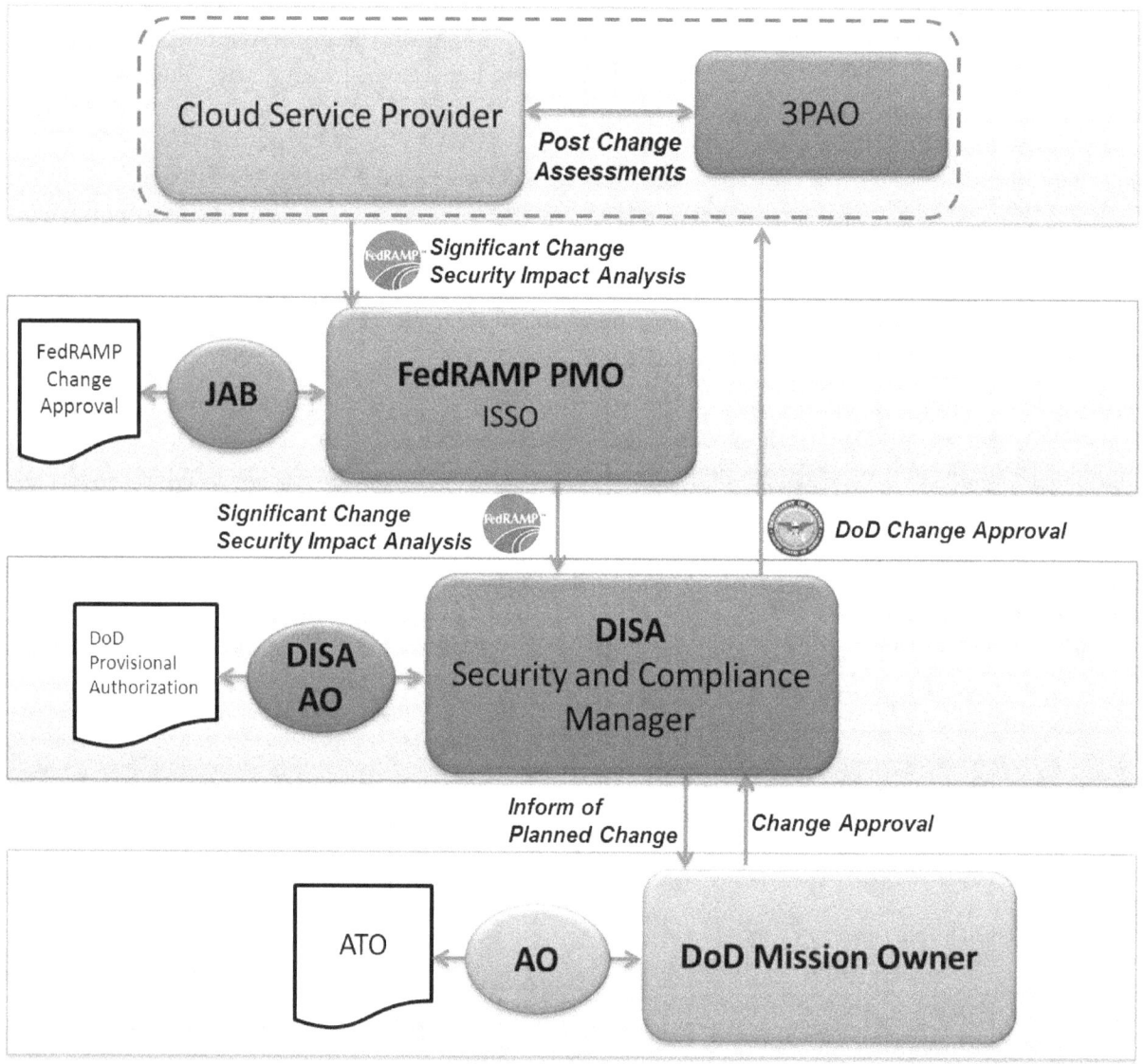

Figure 5 – DoD Change Control Process for CSPs with a FedRAMP JAB PA

Figure 6 shows the normal flow of significant change information if the CSP has a 3PAO assessed Federal Agency ATO listed in the FedRAMP catalog. Since the FedRAMP JAB does not control the Agency ATO, information may not flow from the CSP to the FedRAMP PMO.

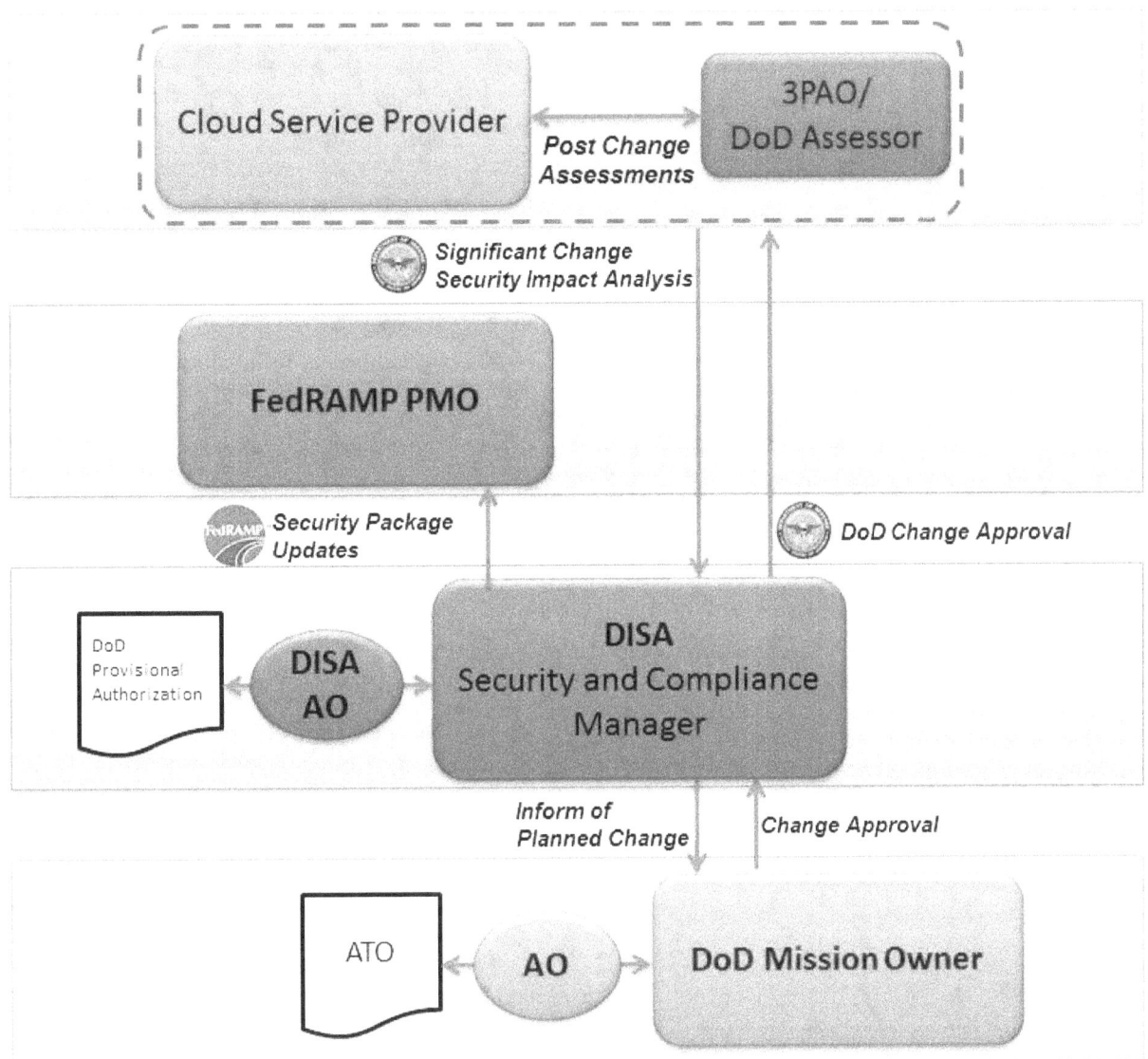

Figure 6 – DoD Change Control Process for FedRAMP CSPs with a 3PAO assessed Federal Agency ATO

5.3.2.2 DoD Self-Assessed CSPs

Figure 7 shows the flow of significant change for non-FedRAMP CSPs having a DoD PA or ATO. The review of significant change information will be directed by the DoD RMF, rather than the FedRAMP change control process. CSPs will have similar responsibilities, but will report directly to DISA. DISA will, in turn, disseminate those artifacts to all Mission Owners utilizing that CSO, the DISA AO, and the CNDSP entities as defined in section 6, "Computer

Network Defense and Incident Response." These entities will review the proposed change to ensure it will not adversely affect the security posture of the CSP with respect its PA or ATO. The planned change will also be reviewed by the Mission Owners consuming the CSP's services for any adverse impact with regard to their specific usage of the CSO.

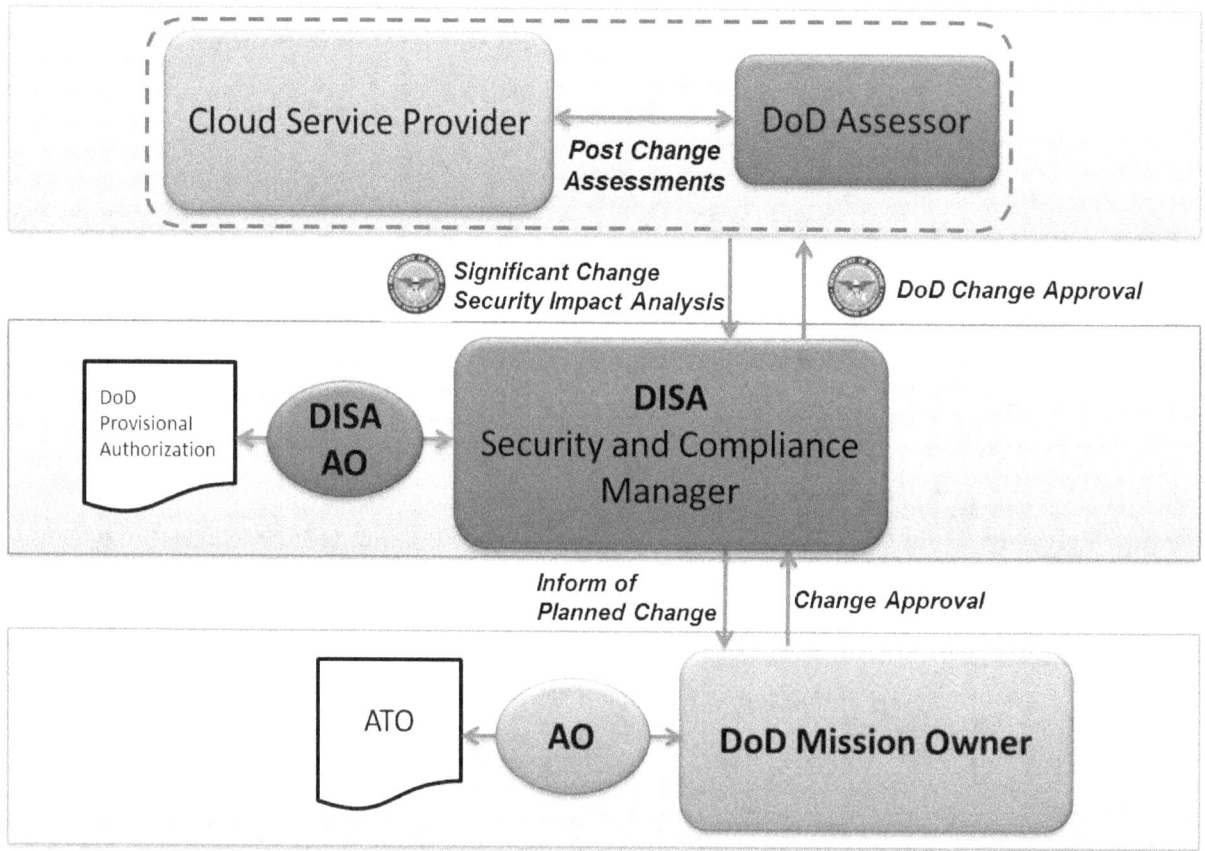

Figure 7 – DoD Change Control Process for DoD Self-Assessed CSPs

5.4   CSP use of DoD Public Key Infrastructure (PKI)

In accordance with FedRAMP's selection of IA-2(12) which states "The information system accepts and electronically verifies Personal Identity Verification (PIV) credentials" and the FedRAMP supplemental guidance which states "Include Common Access Card (CAC), i.e., the DoD technical implementation of PIV/FIPS 201/HSPD-12," CSPs are required to integrate with and use the DoD PKI for DoD entity authentication.

The following sections describe how the CSP fulfills its responsibilities with additional detail in the supporting subsections:

Impact Level 2: Whenever a CSP is responsible for authentication of entities and/or identifying a hosted DoD information system, the CSP will use DoD PKI in compliance with DoDI 8520.03. CSPs will enforce the use of a physical token referred to as the "Common Access Card (CAC)" or "Alt Token" for the authentication of privileged users. CSPs must make use of DoD Online Certificate Status Protocol (OCSP) or Certificate Revocation List (CRL) resources for checking revocation of DoD certificates and DoD Certificate Authorities; and must follow DoD instructions and industry best practices for the management and protection of cryptographic keys.

Impact Levels 4/5: Whenever a CSP is responsible for authentication of entities and/or identifying a hosted DoD information system, the CSP will use DoD PKI in compliance with DoDI 8520.03. CSPs will enforce the use of a physical token referred to as the "Common Access Card (CAC)" or "Alt Token" for the authentication of privileged and non-privileged users. CSPs must make use of DoD OCSP or CRL resources for checking revocation of DoD certificates and DoD Certificate Authorities; and must follow DoD instructions and industry best practices for the management and protection of cryptographic keys. DoD issued PKI server certificates will be used to identify the CSP's DoD customer ordering/service management portals and SaaS applications and services contracted by and dedicated to DoD use.

Impact Level 6: Whenever a CSP is responsible for authentication of DoD entities and/or identifying a hosted DoD information system, the CSP will use NSS PKI in compliance with DoDI 8520.03 and CNSSP-25. CSPs will enforce the use of a physical token referred to as the CNSS Secret Internet Protocol Router Network (SIPRNet) Hardware Token for the authentication of Mission owner and CSP privileged and non-privileged end users. When implementing NSS PKI, CSPs must make use of NSS OCSP or CRL resources for checking revocation of NSS certificates and NSS Certificate Authorities; and must follow CNSS / NSA instructions for the management and protection of cryptographic keys. CNSS issued PKI server certificates will be used to identify the CSP's DoD customer ordering/service management portals and SaaS applications and services contracted by and dedicated to DoD use.

NOTE: A CSP will need to PK enable their customer ordering/service management portals for all service offerings and their SaaS service offerings for general DoD user access at levels 4 and up or provide a customer configurable service offering to permit PK enabling and integration with the required PKI. For complete compliance the CSP will integrate with the DoD PKI and the Federal PKI for levels 2 through 5. For Level 6 the CSP will integrate with the NSS (SIPRNet) PKI. Both the DoD and NSS PKI are operated by DISA[15] while the Federal PKI is operated by GSA[16]. PK enable customer ordering/service management portals may require a separate URL or dedicated application / application interface as best determined by the CSP to meet the Federal Government requirement.

5.4.1 Identification, Authentication, and Access Control Credentials

DoDI 8520.03, *Identity Authentication for Information Systems* is the DoD policy that defines the credentials that DoD privileged and non-privileged users must use to identify themselves to DoD information systems to be authenticated before being granted access. It also defines the credentials that DoD information systems use to identify themselves to each other. This is fully applicable to DoD information systems instantiated on cloud services. Additionally, CNSS Policy #25 and CNSSI 1300 provide similar guidance for NSS. For the purpose of this discussion, the process of identification and authentication will be referred to as I&A.

---

[15] DoD PKI/PKE: http://iase.disa.mil/pki-pke/Pages/index.aspx
[16] Federal PKI: http://www.idmanagement.gov/federal-public-key-infrastructure

UNCLASSIFIED

5.4.1.1 Mission Owner Credentials

This section defines the Mission Owner access control credentials required at each information impact level IAW DoDI 8520.03 in the following categories:

- Mission Owner privileged user access to the CSP's customer ordering and service management interfaces or portals for all service offerings (IaaS/PaaS, SaaS).
  - o Integration with DoD PKI is typically a CSP responsibility. Minimally, the CSP is responsible for providing capabilities that enables Mission Owners to configure a CSP service offering that integrates with DoD PKI.
- Mission Owner Non-privileged user (i.e., mission application end-users) access to CSP SaaS offerings.
  - o Integration with DoD PKI is typically a CSP responsibility. Minimally, the CSP is responsible for providing capabilities that enables Mission Owners to configure a CSP service offering that integrates with DoD PKI.
- Non-privileged user access to Mission Owner's systems and applications instantiated on IaaS/PaaS. (i.e., mission application end-users)
  - o Implementation is a Mission Owner responsibility.
- Mission Owner privileged user access to their systems and applications instantiated on IaaS/PaaS for the purpose of administration and maintenance.
  - o Implementation is a Mission Owner responsibility.

Table 4 lists the Mission Owner credential types required at each impact level and the policy under which they are required.

Table 4 - Mission Owner Credentials

Impact Level	IAW DoD policy	IAW FedRAMP's selection of IA-2(12):
Level 2	▪ Non-privileged user access to publicly released information requires no I&A, unless the information owner requires it. If required, the Mission Owner determines the type of I&A to be used. ▪ Non-privileged user access to non-publicly released non-CUI and non-critical mission information minimally requires I&A through the use of a User Identifier (UID) and password that meets DoD length and complexity requirements. The Mission Owner is encouraged to require the use of a stronger I&A technology in accordance with the sensitivity of the private information (e.g., two-factor token based onetime password, DoD ECA PKI certificate, CAC/PKI, etc.) ▪ Privileged user's access to administer	▪ Mission Owner's privileged user's access to the CSP's customer ordering/service management portals for all service offerings requires the use of DoD CAC/PKI or Alt Token/PKI. DoD ECA PKI certificates may be used by DoD contractor personnel if a physical token cannot be provided. ▪ Non-privileged user access to non-publicly released non-CUI and non-critical mission information in the CSP's SaaS offering minimally requires I&A through the use of a User Identifier (UID) and password that meets DoD length and complexity requirements. The Mission Owner is encouraged to require the use of a stronger I&A technology in accordance with the sensitivity of the private information

	Mission Owner systems/applications instantiated on IaaS/PaaS requires the use of DoD CAC/PKI or Alt Token/PKI. DoD External Certification Authority (ECA) PKI certificates may be used by DoD contractor personnel if a physical token cannot be provided.	(e.g., two-factor token based onetime password, DoD ECA PKI certificate, CAC/PKI, etc.)
Level 4 and 5	▪ Non-privileged user access to CUI, non-CUI critical mission data, and/or unclassified NSS (L5) requires the use of DoD CAC/PKI. DoD ECA PKI certificates may be used by DoD contractor personnel if a physical token cannot be provided. ▪ Privileged user's access to administer Mission Owner systems/applications instantiated on IaaS/PaaS requires the use of DoD CAC/PKI or Alt Token/PKI. DoD ECA PKI certificates may be used by DoD contractor personnel if a physical token cannot be provided.	▪ Non-privileged user access to CUI, non-CUI critical mission data, and/or unclassified NSS (L5) information in the CSP's SaaS offering requires the use of DoD CAC/PKI. DoD ECA PKI certificates may be used by DoD contractor personnel if a physical token cannot be provided. ▪ Mission Owner's privileged user's access to the CSP's customer ordering/service management portals for all service offerings requires the use of DoD CAC/PKI or Alt Token/PKI. DoD ECA PKI certificates may be used by DoD contractor personnel if a physical token cannot be provided.
Level 6	▪ Non-privileged user access to classified information requires the use of NSS SIPRNet Token/PKI. ▪ Privileged user's access to administer Mission Owner systems/applications instantiated on IaaS/PaaS requires the use of NSS SIPRNet Token/PKI.	▪ Non-privileged user access to classified information in the CSP's SaaS offering requires the use of NSS SIPRNet Token/PKI. ▪ Mission Owner's privileged users access to the CSP's customer ordering/service management portals for all service offerings requires the use of NSS SIPRNet Token/PKI.

NOTE: Mission Owner personnel that are involved in managing any portion of a CSP's service offering or who are able to order services from the CSP (i.e., possesses accounts on the CSP's customer ordering and service management interfaces or portals for any service offering (IaaS/PaaS, SaaS)), are considered Privileged Users by DoD and therefore are required to authenticate using DoD CAC or Alt Token IAW DoDI 8520.03.

5.4.1.2 CSP Privileged User Credentials

This section defines the I&A and access control credentials that the CSP privileged users must use when administering CSP CSP's infrastructure supporting Mission Owner's systems.

Impact Levels 2/4: IAW FedRAMP's selection of IA-2(1) and IA-2(3), the CSP must minimally implement two factor authentication for CSP privileged user access to administer and maintain CSP infrastructure supporting Federal and DoD contracted services.

Impact Level 5: IAW DoD policy, the CSP must implement a dedicated strong two-factor I&A capability for CSP privileged user access to administer and maintain dedicated CSP infrastructure supporting DoD contracted services.

Impact Level 6: IAW CNSS policy, the CSP must implement SIPRNet Token/PKI authentication for CSP privileged user access to administer and maintain dedicated CSP infrastructure supporting Federal and DoD contracted services.

5.4.2 Public Key (PK) Enabling

Public Key (PK) enabling refers to the process through which hosts and applications are enabled to hold or use PKI certificates for the following:
- Identifying themselves to other hosts.
- Establishing secure communications paths.
- Accepting DoD PKI certificates for system and user authentication.
- Validating the validity of PKI certificates while making use of the DoD OCSP responder resources and/or CRL resources.

The IASE web site page Public Key Infrastructure (PKI) and Public Key Enabling (PKE)[17] provides information needed to PK-enable Mission Owner's systems/applications instantiated on CSP's IaaS/PaaS offerings and CSP's PK-enabling of SaaS offerings and service ordering/management portals/interfaces.

5.5 Policy, Guidance, Operational Constraints

DoD-specific policy, guidance and operational constraints must be followed as appropriate by CSPs. DISA will evaluate CSP submitted equivalencies to any specific security control, SRG, or STIG requirement on a case by case basis.

5.5.1 SRG/STIG Compliance

CSPs are subject to the FedRAMP selected security control SP 800-53 CM-6. STIGs and/or SRGs may be used to fulfill this baseline configuration requirement.

Impact Level 2: While the use of STIGs and SRGs is preferable, industry standard baselines such as those provided by the Center for Internet Security are an acceptable alternative to the STIGs and SRGs.

---

[17] DoD PKI/PKE: http://iase.disa.mil/pki-pke/Pages/index.aspx

Impact Levels 4/5/6: STIGs are applicable if the CSP utilizes the product the STIG addresses. SRGs are applicable in lieu of STIGs if a product specific STIG is not available. However, the SP 800-53 control applies whether or not a STIG or SRG is available.

CSPs must utilize all applicable DoD STIGs and/or SRGs to secure all DoD contracted cloud computing services provided on dedicated infrastructure that only serves DoD tenants. This applies at levels 4 and above for IaaS, PaaS, and SaaS offerings.

The Mission Owner must utilize all applicable DoD SRGs and STIGs to secure all Mission Owner systems and applications instantiated on CSP's IaaS and PaaS at all levels.

The full list of All STIGs and SRGs can be found on DISA's IASE web site[18].

5.6   Physical Facilities and Personnel Requirements

The following sections discuss facility and personnel requirements as they align to the impact levels.

5.6.1   Facilities Requirements

Impact Level 2: CSP data processing facilities supporting Level 2 information will meet the physical security requirements defined in the FedRAMP Moderate baseline.

Impact Levels 4 and 5: CSP data processing facilities supporting Level 4 and 5 information will meet the physical security requirements defined in the FedRAMP Moderate baseline as well as any FedRAMP+ C/CEs related to physical security.

Impact Level 6: DoD data processing facilities that support cloud services infrastructure and classified service offerings will be housed in facilities (designated as a secure room) designed, built, and approved for open storage commensurate with the highest classification level of the information stored, processed, or transmitted as defined in DoDM 5200.01 Volume 3. DoD Information Security Program: Protection of Classified Information. Commercial CSP's data processing facilities that support cloud services infrastructure and classified service offerings must participate in and be approved through the National Industrial Security Program (NISP) to receive a facilities clearance[19]. The requirements for NISP are outlined in DoD 5220.22M – the National Industrial Security Program Operating Manual (NISPOM)[20]. To receive a DoD PA for Level 6, a CSP must either have a facility clearance or be verified that they can meet the requirements to receive it when a contract is executed.

5.6.2   Personnel Requirements

The concept of cloud operations, given the shared responsibilities between multiple organizations along with the advanced technology being applied within this space, can impact personnel security requirements. The ability for a CSP's personnel to alter the security controls/environment of a provisioned offering and the security of the system/application/data processing within the offering may vary based on the processes/controls used by the CSP. The components of the underlying infrastructure (e.g. hypervisor, storage subsystems, network

---

[18] STIGs and SRGs: http://iase.disa.mil/Pages/index.aspx
[19] DSS Facility Clearance Branch: http://www.dss.mil/isp/fac_clear/fac_clear.html
[20] NISPOM: http://www.dss.mil/documents/odaa/nispom2006-5220.pdf

UNCLASSIFIED

devices) and the type of service (e.g. IaaS, PaaS, SaaS) provided by the CSP will further define the access and resulting risk that a CSP's employee can have on DoD mission or data.

5.6.2.1 Personnel Requirements – PS-2: Position Categorization

The FedRAMP Moderate baseline includes the personnel security controls PS-2, PS-3, and enhancement PS-3(3). Under PS-2, the CSP is required to "assign a risk designation to all organizational positions" and "Establish screening criteria for individuals filling those positions". Supplemental guidance states "Position risk designations reflect Office of Personnel Management (OPM) policy and guidance." The OPM position designation process takes into account the duties, level of supervision, and the scope over which misconduct might have an effect (i.e., worldwide/government-wide, multi-agency, or agency). For IT system and information access it also takes into account the sensitivity level of the information accessed (i.e., non-CUI, CUI, and classified).

The OPM Position Designation Tool is provided to enable Federal Agencies a methodical and consistent means to determine position sensitivity for National Security Positions (e.g., positions concerned with the protection of the Nation from foreign aggression or espionage or positions that require regular access to classified information) and Public Trust Positions (e.g., positions at the high or moderate risk levels, which includes responsibility for protection of information security systems). Position risk levels are determined using the Position Designation Tool. A position may have both National Security and Public Trust considerations that will jointly impact the sensitivity level and ultimately the type of security investigation required. The Position Sensitivity Tool will be used to determine position sensitivity, position risk levels and investigation requirements for key CSP personnel.

DoD's primary concern is CSP personnel with direct access to or can gain access to DoD information, or that have responsibilities that can affect the security of the information technology processing, storing, or transmitting that information. Under OPM policy, such a person with access to CUI or classified information is designated as filling a position designated as "critical-sensitive" or "high risk". However, if the person's "work is carried out under technical review of a higher authority" (i.e., a person holding a "critical-sensitive" or "high risk" position), then the position may be designated as "noncritical-sensitive" or "moderate risk". Positions only having access to non-CUI and publicly released information could have a designation of "non-sensitive" or "low risk". All positions are considered to have some level of "public trust".

From a DoD policy perspective under PS-2 and IAW DoD 5200.2-R, Category I automated data processing (ADP) (ADP-1 or IT-1), positions include those in which an individual is responsible for the planning, direction, and implementation of a computer security program; has major responsibility for the direction, planning and design of a computer system, including the hardware and software; or can access a system during the operation or maintenance in such a way and with a relatively high risk for causing grave damage or realize a significant personal gain. These positions are designated "critical-sensitive". Category II automated data processing (ADP) (ADP-2 or IT-2) positions include those in which an individual may have the same responsibilities listed for ADP-1 but whose work is technically reviewed by a higher authority of the ADP-I category to insure the integrity of the system. These positions are designated "noncritical-sensitive". These designations are in consistent with the OPM Position Designation System October 2010 document[21] and automated tool[22].

To receive a DoD PA, the CSP must demonstrate that their personnel position categorization and compliance with PS-2 is equivalent to the OPM position designations for the similar CSP positions to the "critical-sensitive" (e.g., DoD's ADP-1) or "high risk"; "noncritical-sensitive" (e.g., DoD's ADP-2) or "moderate risk"; and/or "non-sensitive" or "low risk" (i.e., access to only non-CUI and public information) position designations. These designations drive the level of screening to be established IAW the second half of PS-2 and for PS-3.

5.6.2.2 Personnel Requirements – PS-3: Background Investigations

Under PS-3 and PS-3(3), the CSP is required to "Screen individuals prior to authorizing access to the information system", and re-screen IAW an organizational defined frequency. PS-3(3) addresses "additional personnel screening criteria" for information "requiring special protection" such as CUI.

Per the FedRAMP supplemental guidance for PS-3, found in the FedRAMP Control Specific Contract Clauses v2, June 6, 2014 document[23], an agency must stipulate, "IAW OPM and Office of Management and Budget (OMB) requirements", the type of background investigation required for CSP personnel having access to or who can gain access to information. For DoD, the minimum designations are defined by level as follows:

Impact Level 2: CSP personnel supporting Level 2 cloud service offerings will meet the personnel security requirements and undergo background checks as defined in OPM policy IAW the FedRAMP Moderate baseline. As such the minimum background investigation required for CSP personnel having access to Level 2 information based on a "non-sensitive" or "low risk" position designation (i.e., position only has access to public and non-CUI non-critical mission information), is a National Agency Check and Inquiries (NACI). The position sensitivity or risk level and resulting investigation may be elevated beyond the minimum requirement as determined by the Mission Owner / AO, based on additional risk considerations. For instance if the Confidentiality, Integrity or Availability (CIA) of information is determined to be based on a "noncritical-sensitive" or "moderate risk" position using the tool, a National Agency Check with Law and Credit (NACLC) (for "noncritical-sensitive" contractors), or a Moderate Risk Background Investigation (MBI) (for "moderate risk" positions) may be required.

Impact Levels 4/5: CSP personnel supporting Level 4 and 5 cloud service offerings will meet the personnel security requirements and undergo background checks as defined in OPM policy IAW the FedRAMP Moderate baseline, the FedRAMP+ CEs related to personnel security, and DoD personnel security policies. As such the minimum background investigation required for CSP personnel having access to Level 4 and 5 information based on a "critical-sensitive" (e.g., DoD's ADP-1) position designation, is a Single Scope Background Investigation (SSBI) or a

---

[21] OPM Position Designation System document: http://www.opm.gov/investigations/background-investigations/position-designation-tool/oct2010.pdf

[22] OPM Position Designation Tool: http://www.opm.gov/investigations/background-investigations/position-designation-tool/

[23] FedRAMP Control Specific Contract Clauses v2, June 6, 2014; http://cloud.cio.gov/document/control-specific-contract-clauses

Background Investigation (BI) for a "high risk" position designation. The minimum background investigation required for CSP personnel having access to Level 4 and 5 information based on a "noncritical-sensitive" (e.g., DoD's ADP-2) is a National Agency Check with Law and Credit (NACLC) (for "noncritical-sensitive" contractors), or a Moderate Risk Background Investigation (MBI) for a "moderate risk" position designation.

NOTE: To receive a DoD PA for Level 2, 4, or 5, the CSP must comply with the investigation requirements as listed for personnel requiring access to systems and data (e.g. above the hypervisor). Personnel who have access to the CSP infrastructure (e.g. at the hypervisor or below) must comply with OPM investigation requirements or the CSP must demonstrate that their personnel background investigations and compliance with PS-3 and PS-3(3) are consistent with OPM investigation requirements for each position designation.

Impact Level 6: In accordance with PS-3(1), invoked by the CNSSI 1253 Classified Information Overlay, personnel having access to a secure room, the infrastructure supporting classified processing, or handling classified information, in addition to meeting the public trust position suitability/investigation requirements (e.g., a favorably adjudicated SSBI for a system administrator in a DoD ADP-1 position) must have a security clearance at the appropriate level. Systems and network administrators (i.e., privileged users), while typically not approved to handle classified information for need-to-know reasons, are considered to have access to classified information through their duties. Therefore these individuals require a clearance at the appropriate level for the classified information stored, processed, or transmitted

DoD personnel clearances are granted through DoD processes as defined in DoDI 5200.02 and the DoD 5200.2-R, both entitled *DoD Personnel Security Program (PSP)*. Commercial CSPs' personnel clearances are granted through the Industrial Personnel Security Clearance Process[24].

To receive a DoD PA for Level 6, the CSP must either have a facility clearance and cleared personnel who will manage the CSO, or demonstrate the ability to meet the requirements for such as defined in Industrial Personnel Security Clearance Process.

5.6.2.3   Mission Owner Responsibilities Regarding CSP Personnel Requirements

In addition to the above requirements, the FedRAMP Control Specific Contract Clauses v2, also states the following: "Agencies leveraging FedRAMP Provisional Authorizations will be responsible for conducting their own Background Investigations and or accepting reciprocity from other agencies that have implemented Cloud Service Provider systems." It also states Agencies are responsible for the screening process, and may want to stipulate additional screening requirements. As part of the FedRAMP+ assessment, the processes used by the CSP will be evaluated and discussed in the PA as appropriate. DoD Components and/or Mission Owners must review the investigation type required for all position designations and address investigation requirements in their contracts with the CSP.

---

[24] Industrial Personnel Security Clearance Process: http://www.dss.mil/psmo-i/indus_psmo-i_process_applicant.html

UNCLASSIFIED

5.7 Data Spill

Per CNSSI 4009, IA Glossary, a data spill or "spillage" is an unauthorized transfer of classified information or Controlled Unclassified Information to an information system that is not accredited for the applicable security level of the data or information.

A data spill is an incident that requires immediate incident reporting and response from both the Mission Owner and CSP in order to minimize the scope of the spill and the risk to DoD data. Mission owners will report the incident via their normal channels; the CSP must report the spill to the mission/information owner as well as follow the requirements in section 6.4 Incident Reporting and Response. While the Mission Owner will most likely detect a spillage within their own dataset, the CSP might also detect a spillage. CSP detection may depend on a particular service offering where the CSP might have intentional access to the content of a Mission Owner information system.

Cloud environments present a unique challenge for data spill response. Data spills are typically remediated or "cleaned" by sanitizing affected hardware to ensure that reconstruction of spilled data is impossible or impractical. This process, however, frequently requires that affected resources be taken offline until the cleanup is complete. Such loss of availability is not acceptable in a cloud environment with multiple tenants sharing the same infrastructure. CSP use of virtualization and/or innovative storage methods may make physical data locations difficult to ascertain, further complicating spill cleanup.

Variability in CSP infrastructures precludes the possibility of establishing a single cleanup process. Instead, CSPs will be responsible for providing methods and timelines for deleting specified units of data within their infrastructure in a way that provides high assurance that such data cannot be reconstructed. An **example** of such a process is:

- Volatile hardware with subject data will be powered down within 24 hours to clear data, subject to exceptions based on potential side effects of cleanup actions.
- Unencrypted subject data locations on nonvolatile storage hardware will be overwritten or "cleared" as defined in NIST 800-88 within 24 hours, subject to exceptions based on potential side effects of cleanup actions. Encrypted subject data will be deleted cryptographically by destroying the appropriate decryption keys, then "cleared" and overwritten.
- Affected nonvolatile storage hardware will be tracked through required inventory processes and destroyed at the end of its useful life.

NOTE: The examples above are based on currently defined data spill remediation methods for physical systems where the location of the spilled data is likely known. DoD will assess alternative methods for data spill remediation for cloud infrastructures and will approve those deemed acceptable.

CSP's data spill cleanup methods will be evaluated as part of the PA assessment and then made available to all Mission Owners utilizing that CSP. The CSP will be responsible for executing any of those methods upon report of a data spill by a Mission Owner.

Due to data backup and disaster recovery methods used by Mission Owners and CSPs, data spills could affect associated storage. Data spills remediation must extend to storage media where the spilled data might migrate. All backups and mirrored storage affected by the spill must be remediated. Timely detection, reporting, and response are key to limiting the migration of spilled data under these circumstances.

Mission owners must take steps to protect against the detrimental effects of a data spill; to the spilled data, the Mission Owners virtual systems and networks, and to the cloud infrastructure on which it is spilled. One method is to encrypt ALL Mission Owner data stored in a cloud infrastructure. Such encryption must utilize FIPS 140-2 validated data-at-rest cryptography (operated in FIPS mode). If a spillage occurs, the encryption keys to the stored information could be destroyed; requiring data backup, recovery and disaster recovery remediation procedures to restore clean mission data from a clean backup not containing the spilled data. Alternate innovative methods for cloud data spill protection/remediation will be assessed for equivalency to standard methods and approved if found sufficient.

5.8   Data Recovery and Destruction

For the purpose of this section, Data Recovery and Destruction refers to a Mission Owner requiring the recovery and removal of data stored in a CSP's infrastructure for the purpose of transferring it to a different storage facility. Destruction (removal) of the data in the CSP's infrastructure is required subsequent to the successful recovery transfer. Transfers such as these typically occur when the contract with the CSP is terminated for any of several reasons or the CSP goes out of business. Mission owners must prepare for such eventualities and CSPs must support the capability in a timely manner.

Upon request by a Mission Owner, the CSP will make all Mission Owner data stored in certain service offerings available for electronic transfer out of the CSP environment, with subsequent destruction, within 60 days from the date of request. This primarily applies to any service offerings where the Mission Owner cannot just download files and request destruction of the files, as might be the case if the Mission Owner's data is co-mingled in a large database with other Mission Owner's data. Each Mission Owner may also request different means of data transfer (for example, as called out in the SLA), at its discretion. The subsequent destruction of transferred Mission Owner data must include removal from all CSO backups or mirrored storage maintained by the CSP. This is to prevent the Mission Owner data from being restored accidentally or intentionally after destruction has concluded. To support removal/recovery/destruction of CSP customer data in this type of service offering, the CSP must be able to identify Mission Owner data on a mission by mission basis. The CSP will provide assurance of all data destruction.

Alternate timeframes can be proposed and assessed by DoD for acceptability. Data backup entropy (i.e., letting backups be overwritten in accordance with CSP's backup retention and media reuse policies) is unacceptable if longer than the defined destruction time frame. While this approach is typical for IaaS/PaaS, it may not be for SaaS where customer data might be co-mingled in a database and identification of a specific customer's data is most important.

DoD Mission Owners using non-DoD service offerings must be capable of recovery of their data at any time if able to download the data files. For primary storage and CSO-managed backups or mirrored storage (or capability therein even if not obligated by contract) maintained by the non-DoD CSP, Mission Owners must assure that Level 4 and higher data is protected with FIPS 140-2 validated data-at-rest cryptography (operated in FIPS mode). This alleviates the need for data destruction, which can be simply accomplished by destroying the encryption key(s).

5.9 Reuse and Disposal of Storage Media and Hardware

CSPs will ensure that no residual DoD data exists on all storage devices decommissioned and disposed of, reused in an environment not governed by an agreement between the CSP and DoD, or transferred to a third party; as required by the FedRAMP selected security control MP-6.

Impact Levels 4/5: CSPs may not reuse or dispose of storage hardware until all DoD data has been successfully removed. The CSP will minimally ensure this by "Purging" all data on devices prior to decommissioning, disposal, reuse, or transfer, in accordance with NIST 800-88. Devices that are unable to be cleared or purged must be physically destroyed, as defined in NIST 800-88. When there is any doubt to the success of the cleared or purged process, the storage device must be destroyed in accordance with NIST 800-88.

Impact Level 6: CSP's may not reuse or dispose of storage hardware at a lower sensitivity or classification level and will ensure classified data is irretrievable from decommissioned devices by sanitizing them in accordance with NSA/CSS Storage Device Declassification Manual 9-12[25].

5.10 Architecture

This section of the Cloud Computing SRG provides guidance on the various architectural considerations related to DoD's use of commercial cloud services in the following areas:

- The connection between the CSP's infrastructure and the DoD Information Network (DoDIN)
- CSP service protections and integration into required DoDIN CND and access control services
- Mission system/application protections and integration into required DoDIN CND and access control services

5.10.1 Cloud Access Points

The 15 December 2014 DoD CIO memo regarding *Updated Guidance on the Acquisition and Use of Commercial Cloud Computing Services*, states "Commercial cloud services used for Sensitive Data must be connected to customers through a Cloud Access Point (CAP)"

A DoD Cloud Access Point (CAP) is a system of network boundary protection and monitoring devices, otherwise known as an IA stack, through which CSP infrastructure will connect to a DoD Information Network (DoDIN) service; the Non-secure Internet Protocol Router Network (NIPRNet), or Secret Internet Protocol Router Network (SIPRNet). In general, the CAP will provide the following protections:

- Protects the DoDIN and its network services.
- Protects other DoD missions from incidents that affect a particular CSP's supported missions.
- Provides provide perimeter defenses and sensing for applications hosted in the commercial cloud service.
- Provides a point at which Boundary CND sensing will occur.

---

[25] NSA/CSS 9-12:
https://www.nsa.gov/ia/_files/government/MDG/NSA_CSS_Storage_Device_Declassification_Manual.pdf

- Extends the DoD demilitarized zone (DMZ) architecture to external facing mission systems and applications.

The CAP architecture will change character depending on whether the cloud infrastructure is on-premises or off-premises. There are internal CAPs (ICAPs) and DoDIN/NIPRNet/SIPRNet Boundary CAPs (BCAPs). Some CAPs will leverage existing infrastructure and some will be a new capability.

The implementation of the DoDIN BCAP capability is ultimately a DISA responsibility as part of its mission to protect the DoDIN and DoD information. Per the 15 December 2014 DoD CIO memo, initial capability may temporarily be provided by DoD Components other than DISA, as approved by the DoD CIO. Specific CAP architectural requirements (under development) are beyond the scope of this SRG and will be published separately.

Connection of a mission system to the DoDIN via an ICAP or BCAP will be approved and recorded by the DISA Connection Approval Office in accordance with normal connection approval procedures. Initial connections (physical or virtual) to a CSP's network will occur during onboarding of the CSP's first Mission Owner customer. Additional connections will be made or capacity will be scaled as more Mission Owners use the given CSP. Specific processes and procedures regarding connection approval and Mission Owner connections via a BCAP are beyond the scope of this SRG and will be published separately.

CSP Infrastructure (dedicated to DoD) located inside the B/C/P/S "fence-line" (i.e., on-premises) connects via an ICAP. The architecture of ICAPs may vary and may leverage existing capabilities such as the IA Stack protecting a DoD Data center today or may be a Joint Regional Security Stack (JRSS). On the other hand, an ICAP may have special capabilities to support specific missions, CSP types (commercial or DoD), or cloud services.

CSP Infrastructure (shared w/ non-DoD or dedicated to DoD) located outside the B/C/P/S fence-line which connects to the DoDIN/NIPRNet does so via one or more BCAPs. The BCAP terminates dedicated circuits and VPN connections originating within the CSP's network infrastructure and/or Mission Owner's virtual networks. All connections between a CSP's network infrastructure or Mission Owner's virtual networks that is accessed via or from the NIPRNet/SIPRNet must connect to the DoDIN via a BCAP.

Impact Level 2: All traffic to and from off-premises CSP infrastructure serving Level 2 missions and the mission virtual networks will connect via the Internet. The BCAP is not used. On-premises CSP infrastructure serving Level 2 missions and the mission virtual networks will connect via an ICAP. See section 5.10.3.2, "Management Plane Connectivity" for additional details.

Impact Levels 4/5: All DoD traffic to and from CSP infrastructure serving Level 4 and level 5 missions and the mission virtual networks must connect via one or more BCAPs. This includes the production plane for non-privileged user access and the management plane for privileged user access and deployed IA/CND tool connectivity to internal CND monitoring systems. See sections 5.10.2.2, "User/Data Plane Connectivity" and 5.10.3.2 Management Plane Connectivity for additional details. High availability Mission Owner systems and their supporting CSP network infrastructure must connect to two or more BCAPs. The BCAP will support Internet facing Mission Owner systems IAW the DMZ STIG.

UNCLASSIFIED

Impact Level 6: All DoD traffic to and from CSP infrastructure serving Level 6 missions and the mission virtual networks must connect via one or more BCAPs to the SIPRNet instead of the NIPRNet. This includes the production plane for non-privileged user access and the management plane for privileged user access and deployed IA/CND tool connectivity to internal CND monitoring systems. See section 5.10.2.2, "User/Data Plane Connectivity" and 5.10.2.3, "Management Plane Connectivity" for additional details. High availability Mission Owner systems and their supporting CSP network infrastructure must connect to two or more BCAPs.

5.10.2 Network Planes

A plane, in a networking context, is one of three integral components of network architectures. These three elements – the data synchronization/control or network plane, the user/data or production plane, and the management plane – can be thought of as different areas of operations. Each plane carries a different type of traffic and is conceptually an overlay network on top of the network plane.

5.10.2.1 Network Plane Connectivity

The network or data sync/control plane carries signaling traffic and data replication between servers/data centers. Network control packets originate from or are destined for a network transport device (virtual or physical). The network plane in general is subject to network related DoD SRGs and STIGs. This Cloud Computing SRG does not contain additional requirements related to network plane connections to the cloud computing infrastructure.

5.10.2.2 User/Data Plane Connectivity

The user/data plane (also known as the forwarding plane, carrier plane, or bearer plane) carries the network user traffic. Table 5 details the DoD user/data plane connectivity by impact level for DoD on-premises and off-premises CSOs.

NOTE: While this table does apply to non-DoD Federal Government tenants using a DoD on-premises CSO, it does not apply to non-DoD Federal Government tenants using an off-premises CSO that is a Federal Government community cloud having DoD tenants.

Table 5 - User/Data Plane Connectivity

Impact Level	Off-Premises Non-DoD CSP Service Offering Infrastructure	On-Premises DoD and Non-DoD CSP Service Offering Infrastructure
Level 2	▪ User connectivity will leverage commercial infrastructure (i.e., Internet). ▪ Users connecting from the Internet will connect directly while users connecting from inside the DoDIN (i.e., NIPRNet) will connect to the Internet via the DoDIN Internet Access Points (IAPs) then to the CSP infrastructure.	▪ User connectivity will use existing infrastructure (Government owned) for its user/data plane when the user is within the B/P/C/S fence-line (on-premises) and directly connected to the local Base Area Network (BAN) and NIPRNet. ▪ User traffic to/from the NIPRNet to/from the CSO infrastructure will traverse an ICAP. When the user is

	▪ CSO connections will be assessed and authorized using the same external connection requirements as any other Internet-facing connection.	outside the B/P/C/S fence-line (off-premises) connected to the Internet, user traffic must enter/leave the NIPRNet via the DoDIN Internet Access Points (IAPs) then an ICAP via DoD DMZ extension.
Level 4 And 5	▪ DoD and external user connectivity will leverage a DoDIN extension to the commercial facility using government network infrastructure within government boundaries (i.e. NIPRNet) and commercial infrastructure beyond government boundaries (i.e. commercial carrier infrastructure / connectivity service offerings). ▪ The DoDIN extension to a commercial facility can be accomplished with a Multiprotocol Label Switching (MPLS) router and optical switch (referred to as a Service Delivery Node). ▪ The DoDIN extension will traverse a BCAP. ▪ Users connecting from inside the DoDIN (i.e., NIPRNet) will connect via a BCAP while users connecting from the Internet will traverse the IAPs then a BCAP via a DoD DMZ extension. ▪ CSO connections will be assessed and authorized the same as any other internal connection using the same requirements as any other Internet-facing connection (i.e., IAW the DMZ STIG).	▪ CSO connections will be assessed and authorized the same as any other internal connection.
Level 6	▪ User connectivity will leverage a DoDIN extension to the commercial facility using government SECRET network infrastructure within government boundaries (i.e. SIPRNet) and commercial infrastructure beyond government boundaries (i.e. commercial carrier infrastructure / connectivity service offerings). ▪ The DoDIN extension to a commercial facility can be accomplished with a Multiprotocol Label Switching (MPLS) router and optical switch	▪ User connectivity will use existing SECRET network infrastructure (Government owned) for its user/data plane (i.e., SIPRNet). User traffic to/from the SIPRNet will traverse an ICAP. ▪ User traffic to/from the Internet (e.g., executive travel kits users) will use NSA Type 1 encryption or commercial equivalent (CSfC Suite B) and must enter/leave the SIPRNet via the approved gateways. ▪ CSO connections will be assessed and

(referred to as a Service Delivery Node). ▪ The DoDIN extension to a commercial facility will traverse a BCAP and will use NSA Type 1 encryption or commercial equivalent (CSfC Suite B). ▪ User traffic to/from the Internet (e.g., executive travel kits users) will use NSA Type 1 encryption or commercial equivalent (CSfC Suite B) and must enter/leave the SIPRNet via the approved gateways.	authorized the same as any other internal connection using the same requirements as any other Internet-facing connection (i.e., IAW the DMZ STIG).

5.10.2.3 Management Plane Connectivity

The management plane carries network/server/system privileged user (administrator) traffic along with maintenance and monitoring traffic. Table 6 details the management plane connectivity by impact level for Mission Owner's systems/applications and CSP's CSOs.

NOTE: All encryption identified in Table 6, except as stated otherwise, must be accomplished using FIPS 140-2 validated cryptography modules operated in FIPS mode.

Table 6 - Management Plane Connectivity

Impact Level	Mission Owner Management Plane	CSP Service Offering Management Plane
Level 2	▪ **Management connectivity by DoD personnel or DoD contractors from outside the NIPRNet** requires an encrypted, tunneled connection directly via the Internet to the mission system/application and virtual network. Management traffic to CSP service ordering / service management portals must be encrypted if not in an encrypted VPN. Monitoring traffic must be natively encrypted or must traverse a VPN connection. All traffic entering/leaving the NIPRNet must be via the DoDIN Internet Access Points (IAPs). ▪ **Management connectivity from inside the NIPRNet** requires an encrypted, tunneled connection through the NIPRNet to the Internet via the IAPs to manage the mission system/application and virtual network.	▪ **DoD CSP on-premises service offering infrastructure and management:** CSP management connectivity will utilize existing infrastructure such as the Enterprise Services Directorate (ESD) Out of Band (OOB) management network. No service provider security stack is required. ▪ **Non-DoD CSP on-premises service offering infrastructure and management:** The CSP may directly connect their management infrastructure to their service offering infrastructure if collocated. An encrypted, tunneled connection from the CSP's on-premises management infrastructure to the service provider's on-premises service offering infrastructure is also permitted and will be used to access remote service

	Management traffic to CSP service ordering / service management portals must be encrypted if outside an encrypted VPN. Monitoring traffic must be natively encrypted or must traverse a VPN connection. All traffic must enter/leave the NIPRNet via the DoDIN Internet Access Points (IAPs).	offering infrastructure. ▪ **Non-DoD CSP on-premises service offering infrastructure and off-premises management:** CSP management connectivity must leverage an encrypted, tunneled connection from the CSP's off-premises management infrastructure to the service provider's on-premises service offering infrastructure.
Level 4 And 5	▪ **Management connectivity from inside the NIPRNet** requires an encrypted, tunneled connection through the NIPRNet and an ICAP or BCAP to manage the mission system/application and virtual network. Management traffic to CSP service ordering / service management portals must be encrypted if not in an encrypted VPN. Monitoring traffic must be natively encrypted or must traverse a VPN connection. All traffic must enter/leave the NIPRNet via a BCAP ▪ **Management connectivity by DoD personnel or DoD contractors from outside the NIPRNet** requires an encrypted, tunneled connection from the Internet via an IAP and an ICAP or BCAP to the mission system/application and virtual network. Management traffic to CSP service ordering / service management portals must be encrypted if outside an encrypted VPN. Monitoring traffic must be natively encrypted or must traverse a VPN connection via a BCAP and NIPRNet.	▪ **Non-DoD CSP off-premises service offering infrastructure and off-premises management:** CSP management connectivity leverages CSP service offering and management plane infrastructure which should be separate.
Level 6	▪ All management and monitoring connectivity is via the SIPRNet. Management and monitoring traffic will be encrypted using FIPS 140-2 validated cryptography to accommodate separation for Need-to	▪ **DoD CSP on-premises service offering infrastructure and management:** CSP management connectivity will utilize existing SECRET network infrastructure such as the SECRET Out of Band (OOB)

	know reasons.	management network. No service provider security stack is required. ■ **Non-DoD CSP on-premises service offering infrastructure and management:** The CSP may directly connect their management infrastructure to their service offering infrastructure if personnel are collocated using their SECRET LAN. An encrypted, tunneled connection using FIPS 140-2 validated cryptography over SIPRNet from the CSP's on-premises management infrastructure to the service provider's on-premises service offering infrastructure is also permitted and will be used to access remote service offering infrastructure. ■ **Non-DoD CSP on-premises service offering infrastructure and off-premises management:** CSP management connectivity must leverage a SIPRNet extension or a DoD approved encrypted, tunneled connection from the CSP's dedicated SECRET off-premises management infrastructure to the service provider's on-premises service offering infrastructure. ■ **Non-DoD CSP off-premises service offering infrastructure and off-premises management:** CSP management connectivity leverages CSP's dedicated SECRET service offering and management plane infrastructure which should be separate.

5.10.3 CSP Service Architecture

DoD uses the concept of defense-in-depth when protecting its networks and data/information. This includes, but is not limited to, hardening hosts OSs and applications, implementing host firewalls and intrusion detection, strong access control, robust auditing of events, while protecting the networks with application layer firewalls, proxies web content filters, email gateways, intrusion detection / prevention (IDPS), and a De-Militarized Zone (DMZ) /gateway architecture, along with robust network traffic monitoring. The concept must not be lost when moving Mission Owners systems/applications and their data/information to the commercial cloud.

This section details the defense-in-depth security concepts and requirements that both CSPs and Mission Owners must implement to protect DoD data/information and mission systems/applications. Equivalent alternative measures will be assessed by DISA on a case by case basis.

5.10.3.1 CSP Service Architecture - SaaS

Mission Owner use of CSP's SaaS offerings are reliant on the defense-in-depth measures implemented by the CSP for the protection of the service application and the infrastructure that supports it. This includes the protection of all sensitive information stored and processed in the CSP infrastructure. In other words, the Mission Owner relies on the CSP and the security posture of its SaaS offering for the protection of DoD information. During the ATO assessment process for SaaS offerings, defense-in-depth security / protective measures must be assessed for adequacy and potential risk acceptance by DoD. This may be in addition to assessing security controls. The following guidance is reflected in the DoD DMZ STIG and Application Security and Development STIG along with other operating system (OS) and application specific STIGs.

The defense-in-depth security / protective measures to be established by the CSP for SaaS are, but are not limited, to the following:

- Application Layer Firewall (properly configured) and IDPS protection of the CSP's infrastructure supporting the SaaS application offering, as well as segmentation from the CSP's other offerings and corporate networks.
- Application / network architecture which provides unrestricted/restricted DMZ zones with appropriate protections IAW the DoD DMZ STIG for internet/externally facing servers and private / "back end" zones with appropriate protections for application/database servers and other supporting systems/servers.
- Customer data-at-rest encryption protections using FIPS 140-2 validated cryptographic modules operated in FIPS mode.
- Customer data-in transit encryption protections using FIPS 140-2 validated cryptographic modules operated in FIPS mode.
- Hardening / patching / maintenance of OSs and applications. DoD SRGs and STIGS may be used, and must be used if the service is private DoD or a Federal Government Community used by DoD.
- Implement PIV/DoD CAC / PKI authentication for all customer user access on all SaaS offerings that process information at impact Levels 4 and 5 in accordance with IA-2 (12). This includes regular non-privileged users accessing the service and privileged customer users accessing service ordering / management interfaces/portals. SaaS offerings that process information at impact Level 6 must use the CNSS SIPRNet Token.

NOTE: Equivalencies to the vulnerability mitigations provided in DoD SRGs and STIGS may be viable and acceptable but must be approved by the DISA AO.

UNCLASSIFIED

5.10.3.2 CSP Service Architecture - IaaS/PaaS

Mission Owners build systems and applications on virtualized infrastructure provided by the CSO under IaaS/PaaS. There must be a clear delineation of responsibility for security between the CSP and the Mission Owner, which depends on how the CSP presents the security features it supports in the CSO. Under IaaS the Mission Owner is fully responsible for securing the guest operating systems and applications that they build; the CSP will be responsible for securing the virtualization OS (i.e., hypervisor) and supporting infrastructure. Under PaaS, the Mission Owner is fully responsible for securing the guest operating systems and the platform applications and applications that they build. Depending upon how the CSP CSO presents the security features it supports in the CSO, the delineation of responsibility may partially shift from the Mission Owner to the CSP with respect to the guest operating systems and the platform applications. The CSP might take responsibility for securing these areas of a PaaS CSO as part of the core service or as an add-on component.

For the purpose of the remainder of section 5 of this SRG, IaaS and PaaS offerings are generally treated the same with the responsibility of securing the OS and platform applications being that of the Mission Owner. Mission Owners must assess inherited mitigations that the CSP provides to determine that defense-in-depth security / protective requirements are fully met.

CSP IaaS and PaaS offerings must support the defense-in-depth security / protective measures that the Mission Owner must implement to secure the systems and applications that they build on the service offering. These measures are defined in section 5.10.6, "Mission Owner System/Application Architecture using IaaS/PaaS."

5.10.4 IP Addressing and DNS

DoD policy and the Domain Name Service (DNS) STIG require all DoD ISs to use the DoD authoritative DNS servers, not public or commercial DNS servers. Additionally it requires all DoD IS to be addressed in the .mil domain. Mission Owners are not authorized to utilize DNS services offered by the CSP or any other non-DoD DNS provider.

This affects DoD systems instantiated on commercial cloud infrastructure as follows:

Impact Level 2: DoD IS implemented at level 2 will be instantiated in commercial CSP facilities with direct access from the Internet. As such they will be addressed using public Internet Protocol (IP) addresses assigned and managed by the CSP. In order for these systems to comply with DoD DNS policy as noted above, they must use a CNAME in the system's authoritative DNS record within the DoD authoritative servers that directs the URL to the CSP assigned public IP address.

Impact Levels 4/5: DoD IS implemented at levels 4 and 5 instantiated in commercial CSP facilities will be treated and designed as an extension of the NIPRNet, and will be addressed using DoD assigned and managed IP addresses. These systems will use the DoD authoritative DNS servers on the NIPRNet IAW policy as would any other DoD IS. NIPRNet addresses are assigned by the DoD NIC.

Impact Level 6: DoD IS implemented at level 6 instantiated in commercial CSP facilities will be treated and designed as an extension of the SIPRNet and will be addressed using SIPRNet IP addresses. These systems will use the DoD authoritative DNS servers on the SIPRNet IAW policy as would any other SIPRNet connected IS. SIPRNet addresses are assigned by the DoD NIC.

5.10.5 Mission Owner Architecture using SaaS

While defining the SaaS architecture is the responsibility of the CSP, Mission Owners contracting for and using CSP's SaaS offerings must minimally address the following to meet DoD policy:

- Register the Protocols and Services along with their related UDP/TCP IP Ports used by the SaaS service that will traverse the DoDIN. This includes all traffic for Levels 4, 5, and 6 as well as management plane traffic for Level 2.
- Register the service/application with the DoD whitelist for both inbound and outbound traffic.
- Register the CSP's CSO in SNAPS for the connection approval which also includes designation a certified CNDSP as the Tier 2 CND.

As discussed in section 5.10.3, "CSP Service Architecture," the Mission Owner is reliant on the security posture of the CSP and their SaaS offering for the protection of DoD data/information.

5.10.6 Mission Owner System/Application Architecture using IaaS/PaaS

Most of the areas of concern for implementing defense-in-depth security / protective measures that a Mission Owner must address across all information impact levels when implementing systems/applications on IaaS / PaaS include, but are not limited to, the following:

- Implement Virtual Machines (VMs) in one or more virtual networks in which data-flows between VMs, and between VMs and external networks (both physical and virtual) may be controlled.
  NOTE: Virtual networks are typically a feature of the virtualization hypervisor which supports the VMs.
- Implement virtual network(s) in accordance with the approved architecture for the type of application as defined in the DoD DMZ STIG and the Application Security and Development STIG, along with other operating system and application specific STIGs. For example, a web service or application is typically required to have unrestricted/restricted DMZ zones with appropriate protections for internet/externally facing servers and private / "back end" zones with appropriate protections for application/database servers and other supporting systems/servers.
- When infrastructure has direct Internet access, implement virtual application level firewall and virtual IDPS capabilities IAW the applicable DoD SRGs and STIGs to protect the virtual network(s) and interconnected VMs. The Mission Owner and/or their CNDSP must be able to control firewall rules and monitor the virtual network boundary, reporting same to the Tier 1. For dedicated infrastructure with a DoDIN connection (Levels 4-6): implement firewall, IPS, and/or routing methods that restrict traffic flow inbound and outbound to/from the virtual network to the DoDIN connection IAW DoDI 8551. Block all traffic from all other sources such as the CSP's network which is most likely connected to the Internet.
- Implement a secure (encrypted) connection or path between the virtual firewall, the virtual IDS capabilities and the CNDSP responsible for the mission system/application.

See section 6, "Computer Network Defense and Incident Response" for more specific information.

- Harden (STIG) / patch / maintain each VM's OS under IaaS and PaaS IAW DoD policy and CYBERCOM direction. The use of DoD STIGs and SRGs is required for hardening.
- Harden (STIG) / patch / maintain each application provided by the CSP under PaaS IAW DoD policy and United States Cyber Command (USCYBERCOM) direction. The use of DoD STIGs and SRGs is required for hardening.
- Harden (STIG) / patch / maintain each application provided/installed by the Mission Owner IAW DoD policy and USCYBERCOM direction. The use of DoD STIGs and SRGs is required for hardening as is compliance with IAVMs.
- Implement data-at-rest encryption on all DoD files housed in CSP IaaS storage service offerings. A CSP may offer one or more services or methods to accomplish this. Data-at-rest encryption may help mitigate issues with data/information spillage.
- If the DoD information is sensitive government (e.g., FOUO or CUI), FIPS 140-2 validated software crypto modules operated in FIPS mode must be used.
- Implement Host Based Security System (HBSS) IAW DoD policy.
  o Implement HBSS agents on all VMs with a supported general purpose OS.
  o Utilize an HBSS agent control server within NIPRNet.
  o Implement a secure (encrypted) connection or path between the HBSS agents and their control server.
    o Provide visibility by the Mission Owner's CNDSP entities as defined in section 6, "Computer Network Defense and Incident Response."
- Implement scanning using an Assured Compliance Assessment Solution (ACAS) server IAW USCYBERCOM TASKORD 13-670.
  o Implement a secure (encrypted) connection or path between the ACAS server and its assigned ACAS Security Center.
  o Provide visibility by the Mission Owner's CNDSP entities as defined in section 6.
- Implement DoD PKI server certificates for establishing secure connections.
- Implement all required data-in-transit encryption protections using FIPS 140-2 validated crypto modules operated in FIPS mode.
- Implement DoD CAC / PKI authentication as follows:
  o For all privileged user access to VM operating systems and applications for Levels 2, 4, and 5 IAW DoD policy. Level 6 must use the CNSS SIPRNet Token.
  o For all general DoD users of the implemented systems/applications for Levels 4 and 5 IAW DoD policy. Level 6 must use the CNSS SIPRNet Token.
  o Implement a secure (encrypted) connection or path between the implemented systems/applications and the DoD OCSP responders on NIPRNet or SIPRNet as applicable
- Secure Active Directory (AD) (if used) and any associated trusts IAW the DoD Windows OS STIGs and/or other applicable DoD STIGs. This includes trusts between DoD AD forests and CSP CSO AD forests. If such trusts are required, the implementation must be approved by the AO responsible for the DoD AD forest.
- Register the Protocols and Services along with their related IP Ports used by the Mission Owner's system/service/application that will traverse the DoDIN. This includes all traffic for Levels 4, 5, and 6 as well as management plane traffic for Level 2.

- Register the Mission Owner's system/service/application with the DoD whitelist.
- Register the CSP's CSO in SNAP for the connection approval which also includes designating a certified CNDSP as the Tier 2 CND (refer to section 6).

NOTE: Under PaaS (and potentially IaaS) a Mission Owner may contract the CSP to harden (STIG) / patch / maintain VMs, OSs, applications, or maintain STIGed and patched VM images for use if the CSP provides such a service. Such services must be validated to DoD standards IAW all applicable policies (e.g., privileged access). Equivalencies will be assessed and approved on a case by case basis.

6   COMPUTER NETWORK DEFENSE AND INCIDENT RESPONSE

Computer Network Defense (CND) addresses the defense and protection of networks and Information Systems (ISs), detection of threats, and response to incidents. Cyber Situational Awareness (CSA) improves the quality and timeliness of collaborative decision-making regarding the employment, protection, and defense of DoD systems and data. The DoD CND Command and Control (C2) structure provides the means to react to threats and incidents to defend the DoD Information Networks (DoDIN). These are among the key challenges in DoD's adoption of Cloud Service Offerings (CSOs). This section addresses critical CND requirements; tiers, roles and responsibilities; incident reporting and response; and other CND processes.

6.1   Overview of CND Tiers

DoD operates a tiered CND Command and Control (C2) structure as defined in DODI O-8530.2, *Support to Computer Network Defense (CND)*. The structure consists of USCYBERCOM at the top tier (Tier 1) and a network of CND Service Providers (CNDSPs) (Tier 2) that have been accredited by USCYBERCOM IAW DoD policy. Each DoD information system is operated/managed by a Mission Owner (Tier 3) which must be aligned with an accredited CNDSP which monitors and protects the information systems and associated assets. CNDSPs report information to USCYBERCOM which maintains Cyber Situational Awareness over all DoD networks and ISs. USCYBERCOM also provides threat information collected from various sources and threat mitigation orders to the CNDSPs and Mission Owners.

DoD is adjusting its CND C2 structure to include the Joint Force Head Quarters (JFHQ) – DoD Information Network (DoDIN). As the JFHQ moves into operation, certain responsibilities may shift from USCYBERCOM at Tier 1.

6.2   Concept Changes for Tiers for Cloud Computing

With the move to commercial cloud computing, the DoD is adopting a risk-based approach in applying network defense capabilities and processes. As described in section 3, DoD has defined Impact Levels commensurate to the risk and type of data, with each higher level warranting greater protections.

With Impact Level 2 data, the overall value of the data is not mission critical or sensitive in nature, thus it doesn't warrant the same level of protections as higher impact level data. Recognizing that the data at Impact Level 2 has minimal requirements for confidentiality, emphasis must be placed on integrity and availability that achieve a level of security and risk acceptable to the responsible Authorizing Official (AO). User connectivity to the information system flows through the CSP's Internet connection; thus DoD is relying on the network boundary protections and monitoring that the CSP provides for all customers versus capabilities normally provided by a DoD CNDSP. Protection capabilities supporting the mission system at the system/host/application level will be provided by a combination of the CNDSP and the mission system administrators (including the CSP for SaaS).

Level 4 and above data presents greater risk and thus necessitates the need for enterprise defense mechanisms and data collection that enable robust monitoring, event correlation, and analytics. With level 4 and above data, the DoDIN boundary is essentially extended through a connection between the DoD CAP and the CSP's network infrastructure supporting the DoD mission. Therefore, an event may be detected through a few different entities: the CSP through monitoring of their CSO (especially for SaaS); the mission administrators or owners; or the CNDSPs that are supporting the monitoring of the mission and the boundary connection. All entities must work together to quickly investigate and respond to incidents. This change requires new constructs within the CND C2 structure, including the identification of entities with new Tier 2 CND Command and Control (C2) and Operations (Ops) responsibilities. The use of a Cloud Access Point (CAP) drives the requirement for two distinct functions/roles: Boundary CND and Mission CND.

6.2.1   Boundary CND

Boundary CND (BCND) monitors and defends the connections to/from CSPs via an authorized CAP. BCND guards against the risk that each CSP interconnection poses to the DoDIN individually, along with cross-CSP analysis for all connections flowing through an individual CAP. While this function focuses on the connections through a particular CAP, cross-CAP analysis is warranted to determine if a threat extends beyond a single CSP or CAP.

All anomalies identified by a BCND will be forwarded to DISA for cross-CAP analysis activities. The DISA Command Center (DCC) and DISA NetOps Center (DNC) Continental US (CONUS) are assigned global CND C2 and Ops responsibility for protecting the DoDIN. This C2 construct addresses potential impacts across the multiple missions supported by a CSP, ensuring that Mission Owners and supporting MCNDs have access to global situational awareness.

6.2.2   Mission CND

Mission CND (MCND) provides services to a Mission Owner's cloud-based mission systems/applications and virtual networks. Any given MCND may service cloud-based mission systems/applications and virtual networks instantiated in multiple CSPs and multiple CSOs. MCND is not a new Tier 2 entity; rather it is the integration of existing DoD CNDSPs with a focus on elements of cloud computing. The MCND will typically be the CNDSP used by the Mission Owner's Command, Service, or Agency (CSA) for their non-cloud-based ISs; however, Mission Owners can choose to use any certified CNDSP for their MCND provider.

6.3   CND Roles and Responsibilities

The following is a list of the CND C2 functional elements and their responsibilities as it relates to cloud operations.

- **DoDIN CND:** A Tier 1 function of the DCC and DNC CONUS focused on cross-DoDIN risk in DoD's use of cloud computing and commercial CSPs.
  - ○ Responsible for protecting the DoDIN and DoD mission systems in commercial cloud infrastructure through cross-CAP correlation and analysis of events/data.
  - ○ Directs C2 actions regarding DoDIN-wide incident and system health reporting involving a CAP or CSP.
  - ○ For DoDIN-wide incidents, establish and maintain external communications with the CSP and ensure internal DoD communications are established between all entities which include the MCND and BCND.
  - ○ Interfaces with US-CERT to obtain relevant CSP information; ensures cross-sharing of information across all BCND/MCND entities.

UNCLASSIFIED

- **Boundary CND (BCND):** A Tier 1 and Tier 2 function of a certified CND provider responsible for the management and monitoring of a CAP.
  - Responsible for protecting the DoDIN and DoD mission systems in commercial cloud infrastructure connected via the CAP.
  - Coordinates communications between USCYBERCOM and MCNDs.
  - Responsible for monitoring CSP adherence to incident response processes and advising the CSPs via the respective MCND on protecting their infrastructure and the DoD mission systems that they host.
- **Mission CND (MCND):** Tier 2 responsibilities integrated in the existing DoD CNDSPs focused on cloud computing. At a minimum, the MCND is responsible for:
  - Monitoring, protecting, and defending the Mission Owner's cloud-based systems, applications, and virtual networks in the CSP's IaaS/PaaS infrastructure.
  - Ensuring internal DoD communications are established between all entities which include the Mission Owner, MCND, and BCND.
  - Providing information on CSPs and missions being supported and the supporting BCND to DoDIN CND and the JFHQ DoDIN for situational awareness.
- **Mission Administrators:** Administrators of Mission Owner's cloud-based systems, applications, and virtual networks; at a minimum, a Tier 3 entity consuming CNDSP services is responsible for:
  - Following Tier 1 and Tier 2 direction (C2).
  - Maintaining and patching the cloud-based mission systems, applications, and virtual networks.
  - Installing and maintaining protective measures for the cloud-based mission systems, applications, and virtual networks.
- **The CSP:** CSPs provide for their own CND services to provide for a secure environment for Mission Owner's systems, applications, and virtual networks. CSPs will effectively function as an extension of the DoD CND Tier 3 entity (i.e., the Mission Owner) toward this end. At a minimum, CSPs are responsible for:
  - Providing local operational direction and support for CND within their infrastructure and service offerings.
  - Fully maintaining, patching, monitoring, and protecting the infrastructure, operating systems, and applications supporting all service offerings.
  - Fully maintaining, patching, monitoring, and protecting SaaS service offering OSs and applications including DoD data/information in them.
  - And as contracted:
    - Coordinating with the MCND regarding incident response and the mitigation of threats to DoD cloud based mission systems/applications and data.
    - Providing timely incident and system health reports.
    - Maintaining bidirectional Cyber Situational Awareness.
- **Mission Owners:** Individuals/organizations responsible for the overall mission environment, ensuring that the functional and CND requirements of the system are being met. At a minimum, Mission Owners are responsible for:
  - Engaging and funding the services of a MCND to provide for the defense of the Mission Owner's systems, applications, and virtual networks in any CSP's IaaS/PaaS infrastructure (whether DoD operated or operated by a commercial/non-DoD entity).

o Establishing the terms and requirements in the contract with the CSP for incident reporting, incident response, and communications with the appropriate MCND and BCND providers.

Figure 8 provides a graphic representation of these entities and the flow of communications between them.

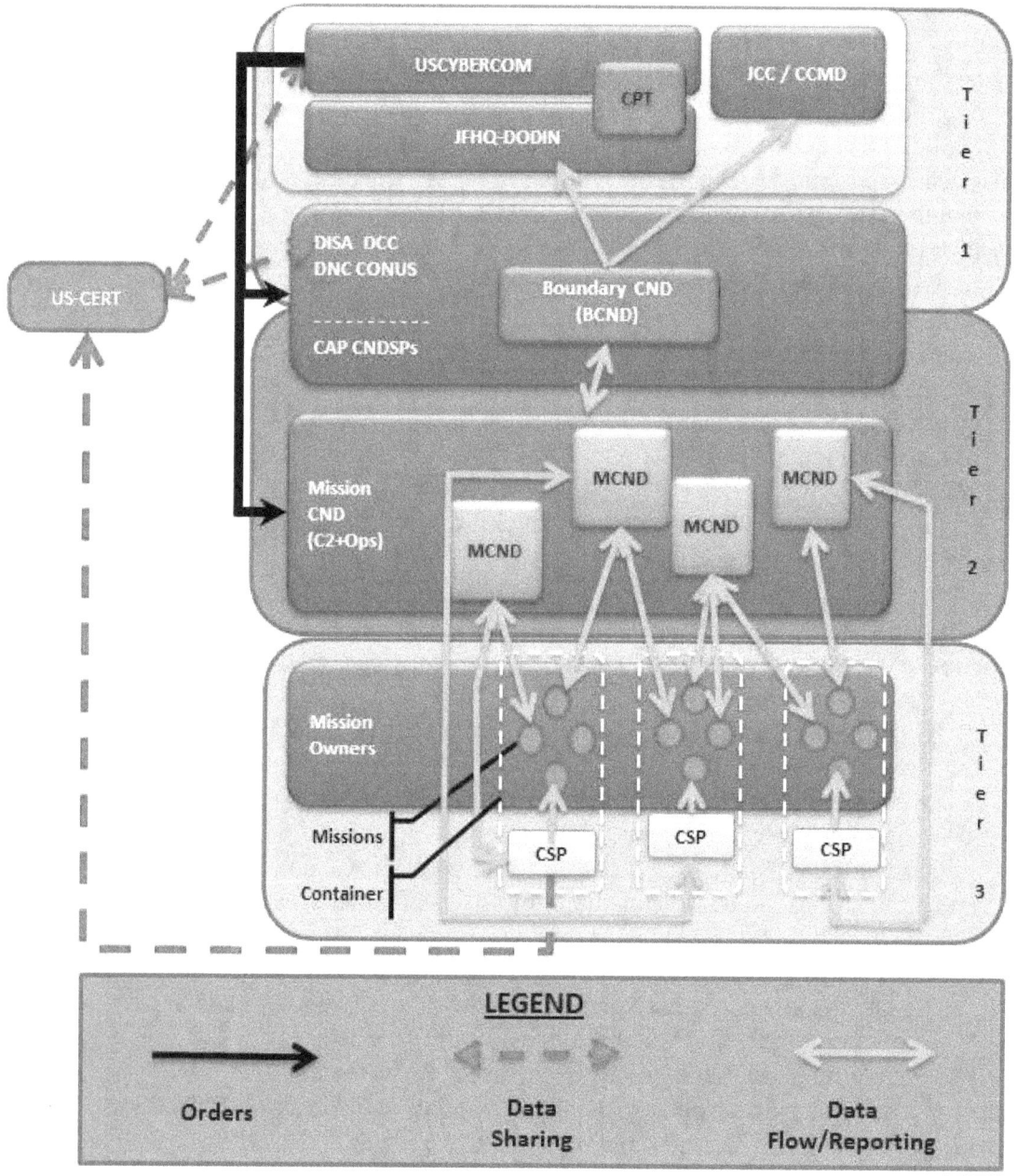

Figure 8 – DoD Cloud Incident Response and CND C2 Structure

6.4   Incident Reporting and Response

FedRAMP, through the selection and implementation of IR-6, requires CSPs to report incidents to the Department of Homeland Security (DHS) United States Computer Emergency Readiness Team[26] (US-CERT) and the consuming Federal Agencies. For CSOs that are multi-tenant or otherwise shared across Federal Agencies outside of the DoD (Impact Levels 2 through 5), incidents will be reported to US-CERT as required by FedRAMP, in parallel with reporting to DoD. For CSPs providing dedicated infrastructure to the DoD (Impact Levels 4 and above), incidents regarding that infrastructure and CSOs will not be reported to US-CERT, but directly to the DoD. The DoD Tier 1 (USCYBERCOM/JFHQ DoDIN) will handle coordination with US-CERT and other entities as appropriate.

All CSPs actively supporting DoD missions will be supported by a MCND. The MCND will be the DoD point of contact to whom the CSP's Operational entity will report and coordinate response to incidents affecting the security posture of the CSP and the CSP's cloud service offerings. The MCND will coordinate with the higher tiered BCND as appropriate.

6.4.1   Incident Response Plans and Addendums

CSPs will provide, either as part of their *Incident Response Plan* or through an *Incident Response Plan Addendum,* their approach to fulfilling integration requirements. CSPs will make their plan or addendum available to DISA for review and approval as a condition of its PA and inclusion in the DoD Cloud Service Catalog. CSPs will update and deliver the *Incident Response Plan Addendum* (if used) in conjunction with updates and deliveries of their *Incident Response Plan,* as required by the FedRAMP selected security control IR-1. A CSP must specifically address data breaches, where a "breach" includes the loss of control, compromise, unauthorized acquisition, unauthorized access, or any similar term referring to situations where any unauthorized person has access or potential access to government data, whether in electronic or non-electronic form, for any unauthorized purpose. CSPs must ensure that the plan or addendum addresses all breaches regardless of the time, day, or location of the breach and must provide for notice to the Government of any breach of its data. The plan or addendum must incorporate any other policies or procedures that the Government may require to be followed in the event of a breach, including, but not limited to:

- How and to whom within the Government, the breach will be reported;
- Specific steps to be taken in order to mitigate or remedy the breach, including time periods for taking such steps (e.g., reporting of Personally Identifiable Information (PII) data breaches within one hour, Negligent Disclosure of Classified Information (NDCIs) which are commonly referred to as spillages);
- How and under what circumstances any individuals or entities affected by a breach will be notified and by whom; and
- Any other special instructions for handling computer security incidents affecting, or potentially affecting U.S. Government data; consistent with guidance and policy directives issued by DoD, NIST, US-CERT and CNSS for incident management, classification, and remediation; or other applicable law, regulation, order, or policy.

---

[26] US-CERT: https://www.us-cert.gov/

UNCLASSIFIED

6.4.2 Information Requirements, Categories, Timelines, and Formats

Defending DoD missions and systems is a shared responsibility that requires all entities (CSPs; CND entities (MCND, BCND); Mission Owners and Mission Administrators) to work collectively as a team. An event may be detected by any of following entities, depending upon the connection architecture (direct Internet or through a CAP):

- CSP personnel through monitoring of their CSO (especially for SaaS);
- Mission administrators or owners (includes the CSP for PaaS/SaaS);
- Supporting MCNDs through their monitoring;
- Supporting BCNDs via the CAP monitoring.

All entities must work together to quickly investigate and respond to events and incidents. In the course of a CSP performing CND for its environments, CSPs will monitor their information systems and report relevant information to the MCND, focused on situations where any unauthorized person has access or potential access to government data.

CSP's reporting requirements to DoD will align with the reporting lexicon used by US CERT for the broader Federal Government reporting requirements. Incident notifications should include a description of the incident and as much of the following information as possible:

- Contract information to include contract number, USG Contracting Officer(s) contact information, contract clearance level, etc.
- Contact information for the impacted and reporting organizations as well as the MCND.
- Details describing any vulnerabilities involved (i.e., Common Vulnerabilities and Exposures (CVE) identifiers)
- Date/Time of occurrence, including time zone
- Date/Time of detection and identification, including time zone
- Related indicators (e.g. hostnames, domain names, network traffic characteristics, registry keys, X.509 certificates, MD5 file signatures)
- Threat vectors, if known (see Threat Vector Taxonomy and Cause Analysis flowchart within the US-CERT Federal Incident Notification Guidelines)
- Prioritization factors (i.e. functional impact, information impact, and recoverability as defined flowchart within the US-CERT Federal Incident Notification Guidelines) (https://www.us-cert.gov/sites/default/files/publications/Federal_Incident_Notification_Guidelines.pdf)
- Source and Destination Internet Protocol (IP) address, port, and protocol
- Operating System(s) affected
- Mitigating factors (e.g. full disk encryption or two-factor authentication)
- Mitigation actions taken, if applicable
- System Function(s) (e.g. web server, domain controller, or workstation)
- Physical system location(s) (e.g. Washington DC, Los Angeles, CA)
- Sources, methods, or tools used to identify the incident (e.g. Intrusion Detection System or audit log analysis)
- Any additional information relevant to the incident and not included above.

Initial incident reports should be submitted within one hour of discovery with follow-on information provided as available. Initial reports may be incomplete to facilitate communication and teamwork between the CSP and the supporting MCND/BCND entities. CSPs should balance the necessity of timely reporting (incomplete reports with critical information) versus complete reports (those with all blocks completed). Timely reporting is vital, and complete information should follow as details emerge.

NOTE: These requirements are applicable to all systems at all Information Impact Levels. The CSP must follow these requirements when integrating with the DoD Command and Control (C2) and Network Operations (NetOps) structure. Mission Owners must include these requirements in the contract, even at Level 2.

6.4.3 Incident Reporting Mechanism

DoD CSP's CND providers will report all incidents IAW normal DoD processes using the Joint Incident Management System (JIMS).

Commercial CSPs will report all incidents via the on-line Defense Industrial Base (DIB) Cyber Incident Collection Form (ICF)[27]. Use of the on-line form is preferred. Access to this form requires a DoD-approved medium assurance External Certificate Authority (ECA) certificate. If you are unable to access this form, please call (877) 838-2174 or email: DCISE@DC3.mil.

The CSP must include, for routing purposes, all MCND points of contact (POCs) for all DoD missions affected by the incident. This is in addition to any other POCs required by the tool for routing to contract managers, etc. The MCND, once the report is received, will initiate the DoD reporting process via JIMS.

Note: The Incident Collection Form (ICF) requires modification in order to be fully aligned with the above reporting requirements. In the interim the current form will be used. CSPs should complete the fields as appropriate.

When classified incident reporting is appropriate and directed, CSPs will use SIPRNet email or secure phone/fax to report and coordinate incidents as specified. This will always be the case for Level 6 reporting.

Existing notification mechanisms of a CSP that are already in place to communicate between the CSP and its customers for some or all classes of CND information may be used, as long as those mechanisms demonstrate a level of assurance, equivalent to the listed encrypted mechanisms, for the confidentiality and integrity of the information.

6.5 Warning, Tactical Directives, and Orders

The DoD operates a tiered CND C2 structure in order to effectively defend DoD information systems that are networked globally across a diverse set of environments. Each of these environments must defend the network and ensure the security of computing and communication systems. It is critical that certain information be disseminated and that actions and supporting countermeasures can be directed from higher levels of command to network defenders (which include CSPs supporting defense of their CSOs).

---

[27] DIBNet CS/IA Portal: http://dibnet.dod.mil/staticweb/index.html

The DoD cyber chain of command for CSPs is represented in Figure 8 (Section 6.3). USCYBERCOM, at Tier 1, disseminates Warnings, Tactical Directives, and Orders to both the BCND and MCNDs (all Tier 2). The BCND entities will analyze them for their applicability to individual CSPs, and then communicate with USCYBERCOM and the CSPs as appropriate. CSPs (effectively acting as Tier 3) will coordinate with the BCND, MCND, and Mission Owners as contracted to implement the provided guidance and countermeasures.

CSPs must be able to receive, act upon, and report compliance with directives and notifications sent by CND Tier 2 (MCND or BCND), as required by FedRAMP selected security control SI-5.

6.6   Continuous Monitoring / Plans of Action and Milestones (POA&Ms)

Understanding existing vulnerabilities and risks within the enterprise is a key component in performing effective CND analysis. The vulnerability reports and POA&Ms developed by the CSPs as part of continuous monitoring requirements supporting both FedRAMP and FedRAMP+ requirements will be made available by DISA's cloud services support team to the MCND and BCND providers for their collective use in providing CND.

6.7   Notice of Scheduled Outages

Planned outages affecting mission systems are to be coordinated through the Mission Owner; with the goal of minimizing impacts to the operational community. An approved outage is referred to as an Authorized Services Interruption (ASI). CSPs must notify all affected MCND providers of ASIs under their control when an outage starts and upon return to service. Outages or changes that affect more than one mission environment must be reported by the MCND to the BCND to enable broader situational awareness across all MCND providers. Mission owners and administrators are responsible for the same notifications to the MCND when the ASI is under their control.

6.8   PKI for CND Purposes

The DoD PKI program provides assurances of an individual's identity, which is important in sharing information regarding C2 and CND functions. This section outlines requirements for establishing trusted identities for CSP personnel communicating securely with DoD CND personnel.

Impact Level 2 through 5: CSPs must preferably have either a DoD PKI certificate or a DoD-approved External Certification Authority (ECA) medium-assurance PKI Certificate[28] for each person that needs to communicate with DoD via encrypted email. The DoD has established the ECA program to support the issuance of DoD-approved certificates to industry partners and other external entities and organizations; providing a mechanism to securely communicate with the DoD and authenticate to DoD Information Systems. Additional information on the ECA program can be found at http://iase.disa.mil/pki/eca/Pages/index.aspx. Equivalent alternative measures will be assessed on a case by case basis.

Impact Level 6: CSPs serving Level 6 systems will already have SIPRNet tokens / NSS PKI certificates for their system administrators by virtue of the connection to SIPRNet. Incident

---

[28] DoD ECA PKI certificate: http://iase.disa.mil/pki/eca/Pages/index.aspx

UNCLASSIFIED

response and CND personnel will use SIPRNet tokens/certificates to communicate with DoD via encrypted email.

6.9   Vulnerability and Threat Information Sharing

Vulnerability and threat information sharing is a highly effective way for DoD to help CSPs protect and defend DoD information housed or processed in their service offerings. Government sources such as US CERT and USCYBERCOM provide detailed vulnerability information. Several commercial sources also provide supplemental information that can be used by CSPs in further defending their infrastructure. CSPs are encouraged to leverage such knowledge sources. However, much of the information that the DoD can provide to CSPs is classified. An avenue to obtain such information follows:

The Defense Industrial Base Cyber Security / Information Assurance Program[29] (DIB CS/IA) is a program to enhance and supplement DIB participants' capabilities to safeguard DoD information that resides on, or transits, DIB unclassified information systems. Membership in DIB CS/IA enables DIB participants to acquire access to DIBNet-U and DIBNet-S, the unclassified and classified networks used for data sharing and collaboration. Access to DIBNet provides CSPs with access to CYBERCOM notifications, classified email, and the DIB web portals.

Access to DIBNet provides CSPs with access to both classified and unclassified cyber threat information, including mitigation strategies. DIB CS/IA program membership is voluntary, although cyber incident reporting as described in section 6.4.3 is mandatory. Eligible CSPs are encouraged to join the voluntary DIB CS/IA program to facilitate their protection of infrastructure that hosts higher-value DoD data and systems.

NOTE: DoD CSPs are already integrated into the CND communications architecture and receive unclassified CYBERCOM notifications via established channels.

---

[29] DIBNet CS/IA Portal: http://dibnet.dod.mil/staticweb/index.html

This page is intentionally blank.

Appendix A References

1. Executive Order 13526: Classified National Security Information, dated 29 December 2009.
   http://www.archives.gov/isoo/policy-documents/cnsi-eo.html

2. Executive Order 12829 – National Industrial Security Program, dated January 1993.
   http://www.archives.gov/isoo/policy-documents/eo-12829.html

3. NIST SP 500-292: NIST Cloud Computing Reference Architecture, dated September 2011.
   http://www.nist.gov/customcf/get_pdf.cfm?pub_id=909505

4. NIST SP 800-53: Recommended Security Controls for Federal Information Systems and Organizations, Revision 4, dated April 2013.
   http://nvlpubs.nist.gov/nistpubs/SpecialPublications/NIST.SP.800-53r4.pdf

   Note: http://csrc.nist.gov/publications/PubsSPs.html contains additional documents relating to SP 800-53.

5. NIST SP 800-59: Guideline for Identifying an Information System as a National Security System, dated August 2003.
   http://csrc.nist.gov/publications/nistpubs/800-59/SP800-59.pdf

6. NIST SP 800-66, Revision 1: An Introductory Resource Guide for Implementing the Health Insurance Portability and Accountability Act (HIPAA) Security Rule, dated October 2008.
   http://csrc.nist.gov/publications/nistpubs/800-66-Rev1/SP-800-66-Revision1.pdf

7. NIST SP 800-88, Revision 1: Draft: Guidelines for Media Sanitization, dated September 2012.
   http://csrc.nist.gov/publications/drafts/800-88-rev1/sp800_88_r1_draft.pdf

8. NIST SP 800-122: Guide to Protecting the Confidentiality of Personally Identifiable Information (PII), dated April 2010.
   http://csrc.nist.gov/publications/nistpubs/800-122/sp800-122.pdf

9. NIST SP 800-144: Guidelines on Security and Privacy in Public Cloud Computing, dated December 2011.
   http://csrc.nist.gov/publications/nistpubs/800-144/SP800-144.pdf

10. NIST SP 800-145: The NIST Definition of Cloud Computing, dated September 2011.
    http://csrc.nist.gov/publications/nistpubs/800-145/SP800-145.pdf

11. NIST SP 800-37, Revision 1: Guide for Applying the Risk Management Framework to Federal Information Systems, dated February 2010.
    http://csrc.nist.gov/publications/nistpubs/800-37-rev1/sp800-37-rev1-final.pdf

12. **CNSS Instruction 4009: National Information Assurance (IA) Glossary, dated 30 April 2010. .**
https://www.cnss.gov CNSS Instruction 1253: Security Categorization and Control Selection for National Security
Systems, dated 27 March 2014.
https://www.cnss.gov

13. CNSS Instruction No.1253F, Attachment 5: Classified Information Overlay dated 09 May 2014.
https://www.cnss.gov

14. CNSS Instruction No.1253F, Attachment x: Privacy Overlay dated TBD.
https://www.cnss.gov (when available)

15. DoD Chief Information Officer, Updated Guidance on the Acquisition and Use of Commercial Cloud Computing Services, 15 December 20014.
http://iase.disa.mil/Documents/commercial_cloud_computing_services.pdf

16. DoD Instruction 8500.01: Cybersecurity, dated 14 March 2014.
http://dtic.mil/whs/directives/corres/pdf/850001_2014.pdf

17. DoD Instruction 8510.01: Risk Management Framework (RMF) For DoD Information Technology (IT), dated 12 March 2014.
http://dtic.mil/whs/directives/corres/pdf/851001_2014.pdf

18. DoD Instruction 8520.03: Identity Authentication for Information Systems, dated 13 May, 2011.
http://dtic.mil/whs/directives/corres/pdf/852003p.pdf

19. DoD Instruction O-8530.2, "Support to Computer Network Defense (CND)", March 9, 2001.
https://whsddpubs.dtic.mil/corres/pdf/O85302p.pdf (PKI requiredd)

20. DoD Instruction 5220.22: National Industrial Security Program, dated March 2011.
http://www.dtic.mil/whs/directives/corres/pdf/522022p.pdf

21. DoD Instruction 5200.02: DoD Personnel Security Program (PSP), Change 1 dated September 2014
http://www.dtic.mil/whs/directives/corres/pdf/520002_2014.pdf

22. DoD Manual 5220.22 Manual: National Industrial Security Program: Operating Manual (NISPOM), dated march 2013.
http://www.dtic.mil/whs/directives/corres/pdf/522022m.pdf

23. DoD Instruction 5200.01: DoD Information Security Program and Protection of SCI, dated June 2011.
http://www.dtic.mil/whs/directives/corres/pdf/520001p.pdf

24. DoD Manual 5200.01 Vol 1: DoD Information Security Program: Overview, Classification and Declassification, dated February 2012.
http://www.dtic.mil/whs/directives/corres/pdf/520001_vol1.pdf

UNCLASSIFIED

25. DoD Manual 5200.01 Vol 2: DoD Information Security Program: Marking of Classified Information, dated March 2013.
http://www.dtic.mil/whs/directives/corres/pdf/520001_vol2.pdf

26. DoD Manual 5200.01 Vol 3: DoD Information Security Program: Protection of Classified Information, dated March 2013.
http://www.dtic.mil/whs/directives/corres/pdf/520001_vol3.pdf

27. DoD Manual 5200.2-R: Personnel Security Program, dated February 1996.
http://www.dtic.mil/whs/directives/corres/pdf/520002r.pdf

28. CJCSM 6510.01B: Chairman of the Joint Chiefs of Staff Manual: Cyber Incident Handling Program, dated 10 July 2012.
http://www.dtic.mil/cjcs_directives/cdata/unlimit/m651001.pdf

29. DSS Facility Clearance Branch
http://www.dss.mil/isp/fac_clear/fac_clear.html

30. DoD ECA PKI Certificate:
http://iase.disa.mil/pki/eca/Pages/index.aspx

31. OPM Position Designation System 2010: .
http://www.opm.gov/investigations/background-investigations/position-designation-tool/oct2010.pdf

32. Federal Risk and Authorization Management Program (FedRAMP) Home Page
http://cloud.cio.gov/fedramp

33. FedRAMP Control Specific Contract Clauses v2, June 6, 2014; http://cloud.cio.gov/document/control-specific-contract-clauses

34. Defense Information Systems Agency, the Security Technical Implementation Guide (STIG) Home Page.
http://iase.disa.mil

35. Defense Information Systems Agency, DoD Cloud Services Support website.
http://disa.mil/Services/DoD-Cloud-Broker

This page is intentionally blank.

Appendix B   Definitions

Authenticity: The property of being genuine and being able to be verified and trusted; confidence in the validity of a transmission, a message, or message originator.

Availability: The property of being accessible and useable upon demand by an authorized entity.

Classified Data: Information that has been determined: (i) pursuant to Executive Order 12958 as amended by Executive Order 13292, or any predecessor Order, to be classified national security information; or (ii) pursuant to the Atomic Energy Act of 1954, as amended, to be Restricted Data (RD).

CNDSP: Computer Network Defense Service Provider

Federal Community Cloud: A multi-tenant cloud in which services are provided for the exclusive use of the DoD and Federal Government organizations. Resources providing the cloud services must be dedicated to Federal Government use and require physical separation from non-DoD/non-Federal customers.

Confidentiality: The property that information is not disclosed to system entities (users, processes, devices) unless they have been authorized to access the information.

Infrastructure as a Service (IaaS): A cloud service model focused on providing infrastructure required to host a workload; includes virtual machines, servers, storage, load, balancers, network, etc.

Integrity: The property whereby an entity has not been modified in an unauthorized manner.

JAB: Joint Authorization Board. The primary governance and decision-making body for the FedRAMP program.

Non-Repudiation: Assurance the sender of data is provided with proof of delivery and the recipient is provided with proof of the sender's identity, so neither may later deny having processed the data.

Platform as a Service (PaaS): A cloud service model focused on providing a suite of environment capabilities that enables the execution or development of applications; includes operating system, execution runtime, database, web server, development tools, etc.

Private Cloud: Cloud in which services are provided for the exclusive use of the DoD; supporting multiple DoD tenants or DoD sponsored tenants in the same cloud. The DoD maintains ultimate authority over the usage of the cloud services, and any non-DoD use of services must be authorized and sponsored through the DoD. Resources providing the cloud services must be dedicated to DoD use and have physical separation from resources not dedicated to DoD use.

Restoration: The return of something to a former, original, normal, or unimpaired condition.

Software as a Service (SaaS): A cloud service model focused on providing the full suite of products and applications to provide a service; includes email, virtual desktop, communication, applications, etc.

This page is intentionally blank.

UNCLASSIFIED

Appendix C   Roles and Responsibilities

Table 7 provides a summary of the major roles and responsibilities in implementation of the Cloud Computing SRG.

Table 7 - Roles and Responsibilities

Role	Responsibility
DISA	• Provide security requirements guidelines (SRGs) and Security Technical Implementation Guidance (STIGs) for DoD cloud computing • Assess CSP's Service Offerings and 3PAO results for consideration in awarding a DOD Provisional Authorization • Issue DoD Provisional Authorizations • Develop and maintain a DoD Cloud Access Point (CAP). • Provide DoDIN Computer Network Defense (CND) capabilities and maintain a CND concept of operations (CONOPS). • Provide technical support for the DoD CIO's role on the FedRAMP Joint Authorization Board • Provide a catalog of DoD cloud services . • Maintain a registry of DoD Components using commercial cloud services. • Support the DoDIN Waiver Process. • Receives CSP's continuous monitoring products and passes them to the appropriate entities within DoD • Serve as the DoD CNDSP certifier
Cloud Service Provider (CSP)	• Commercial vendor or Federal organization offering or providing cloud services (Includes DoD CSPs) • Provides Cloud Service Offerings for mission use • Provides CNDSP services (all tiers) for their infrastructure and service offerings
Cloud Access Point (CAP)	• Provided by DISA or other DoD Component • Protect DoD missions from vulnerabilities or risk that may affect operations in a CSP environment • Provide perimeter defenses and sensing for applications hosted in the commercial cloud service
DoD Chief Information Officer (DoD CIO)	• Official approving authority for all CAPs
FedRAMP Joint Authorization Board (JAB)	• Reviews CSP security assessment packages under the FedRAMP program • Grants FedRAMP Provisional Authorizations

Role	Responsibility
Third Party Assessment Organizations (3PAO)	• Independently performs security assessments of a CSP cloud offering and creates security assessment package artifacts in accordance with FedRAMP requirements • May perform continuous monitoring of CSP systems • Independently assesses a CSP's compliance to DoD FedRAMP+ security controls and other requirements
DISA Authorizing Official (AO)	• Official approving PA for a CSP's Service Offerings for DoD use
DISA CND Functions	• Perform cross-CAP correlation and analysis of event/data. • Direct C2 actions regarding DoDIN-wide incident and system health reporting involving a CAP or CSP. • For DoDIN-wide incidents, establish and maintain external communications with the CSP and ensure internal DoD communications are established between all entities which include the MCND and BCND. • Interface with US-CERT to obtain relevant CSP information; ensures cross-sharing of information across all BCND/MCND entities.
DoD Component Authorizing Official (AO)	• Official approving ATOs for Mission Owner's systems/applications • Reviews PA documentation to understand residual risk
Mission Owner (CSP's DoD Cloud Customer DoD Cloud Consumer)	• DoD entity that acquires cloud services in support of its mission • Performs assessment to issue ATO for their mission systems/applications • Ensures Tier 2 Mission Computer Network Defense (MCND) Service Provider is identified and funded • Serves as CND Tier 3 for their mission systems/applications • Ensures CSP requirements for CND and other SRG requirements are included in any cloud contracts
Department of Homeland Security (DHS) United States Computer Emergency Readiness Team (US-CERT)	• Receives incident reports from CSP as mandated by FedRAMP. • Responsible for coordination across non-DoD agencies
Computer Network Defense Service Provider (CNDSP)	• Provides Computer Network Defense (CND) services and Command and Control (C2) direction addressing the protection of the network, detection of threats, and response to incidents.

Role	Responsibility
United States Cyber Command (USCYBERCOM) / JFHQ-DODIN • DoD Tier 1 CNDSP	• Notify and Coordinate as appropriate with US-CERT, Intelligence Community, Law Enforcement, and other Federal Agencies • Provides Computer Network Defense (CND) services and Command and Control (C2) direction for the entire DoDIN and all DoD information systems
Boundary CND (BCND) • DoD Tier 2 CNDSP	• Monitors and defends the connections to/from off-premises CSPs at the Cloud Access Point (CAP) • Provides cross-CSP analysis capabilities or entities • Communicates with CND Tier 1 and Tier 2 entities
Mission CND (MCND) • DoD Tier 2 CNDSP	• Provides CND / C2 services to specific Mission Owner's systems/applications and virtual networks • Serves as the DoD CND / C2 point of contact for the CSP • Communicates with CND Tier 2 and Tier 3 entities

www.ingramcontent.com/pod-product-compliance
Lightning Source LLC
Chambersburg PA
CBHW081236280526
45787CB00006B/2678